America's Mayor

America's Mayor:
The Hidden History of
Rudy Giuliani's New York

Edited by
Robert Polner

With a Preface by
Jimmy Breslin

Cover art by Zhou Tiehai, courtesy of the artist and Shanghart Gallery
Cover by David Janik

Published by Soft Skull Press
55 Washington Street, 804
Brooklyn, New York 11201
www.softskull.com

Distributed by Publishers Group West
www.pgw.com | 1.800.788.3123

Printed in Canada

Library of Congress Cataloging-in-Publication Data

America's mayor : the hidden history of Rudy Giuliani's New York / edited by
Robert Polner.
    p. cm.
  ISBN 1-932360-58-1 (alk. paper)
  1. Giuliani, Rudolph W. 2. Giuliani, Rudolph W.—Political and social
views. 3. New York (N.Y.)—Politics and government—1951– I. Polner, Rob.
  F128.57.G58A47 2005
  974.7'1043'092—dc22

                            2005003350

Contents

For Monica

Contributors

ROBERT POLNER is a reporter for *Newsday*. He was a 2004–2005 Annenberg Fellow in 9/11 Security and Liberty at the University of Southern California and has won numerous journalism awards. His articles have appeared in several magazines, among them *Progressive*, *City Limits*, and *Columbia Journalism Review*, and he has taught news writing at New York University and Columbia University's Graduate School of Journalism. He was assistant city editor for *Newsday*'s Pulitzer Prize–nominated coverage of the Blackout of 2003, and reported for the paper's Pulitzer-winning coverage of the crash of TWA Flight 800 off Long Island in 1996. During much of the Giuliani mayoralty, he reported on politics and government at New York's City Hall. He is the co-author (with Paul Schwartzman) of *New York Notorious: A Borough-by-Borough Tour of the City's Most Infamous Crime Scenes* (1992).

CHARLES V. BAGLI is a staff writer at the *New York Times*, covering the intersection of politics and real estate in New York. He has previously reported for the *New York Observer*, the *Daily Record* of Parsippany, NJ, the *Tampa Tribune*, and the *Nation*. He has also worked as a transit bus driver, roofer, and furnace tender.

KEVIN BAKER is the author of *Sometimes You See it Coming* (1993), a novel based loosely on the life of Ty Cobb; *Dreamland* (1999); *Paradise Alley* (2002); and *Strivers Row*, which will be published in the spring of 2006 and will complete his City of Fire trilogy. Baker was chief historical researcher for Harold Evans's best-selling history, *The American Century*, published in 1999. He writes the "In the News" column for *American Heritage* magazine, and his work has appeared in such publications as the *New York Times*, *Washington Post*, *Chicago Tribune*, *Los Angeles Times*, *Frankfurter Rundschau*, *Harper's Magazine*, *Talk*, and *Industry Standard*.

KATHLEEN BRADY writes frequently about New York City. A former reporter for *Time* magazine, she was named a Fellow of the Society of American Historians for her biographical work, *Ida Tarbell: Portrait of a Muckraker.*

JIMMY BRESLIN is a columnist who has appeared regularly in various newspapers in New York City, most recently *Newsday*. He won the 1986 Pulitzer Prize for commentary. Breslin is the author of a biography of Damon Runyon and several novels and nonfiction works, including *The Gang That Couldn't Shoot Straight*. His book, *The Short Sweet Dream of Eduardo Gutierrez*, about an immigrant worker who died at a Brooklyn construction site, was published in 2000.

JERRY CAPECI is a leading expert on the Mafia and has reported for the *New York Daily News* and the *New York Post*. He writes "Gang Land," an award-winning column that runs in the *New York Sun* and online at www.ganglandnews.com. He has written several books about organized crime. His latest, *The Complete Idiot's Guide to the Mafia, Second Edition*, was published by Alpha Books in 2005.

GLENN CORBETT is an assistant professor of fire science at John Jay College of Criminal Justice at the City University of New York. He is an assistant chief in the Waldwick, New Jersey, fire department, the technical editor of *Fire Engineering* magazine, and former president of the New Jersey Society of Fire Service Instructors. He also serves on the Federal Advisory Committee to the National Institute of Standards and Technology.

NEIL DEMAUSE is a regular contributor to the *Village Voice* and co-author of *Field of Schemes: How the Great Stadium Swindle Turns Public Money into Private Profit* (1999). His *In These Times* article on welfare reform, "Bad to Worse," was honored by Project Censored as one of the top censored media articles of 2003–03.

JIM DWYER, a native New Yorker, has written about the city for more than twenty years in articles, columns, and books. He currently works at the *New York Times*.

Contributors

LYNNELL HANCOCK is an award-winning education journalist and a professor in the Graduate School of Journalism at Columbia University. She has worked as a reporter at *Newsweek*, the *Village Voice*, and the *New York Daily News*. She is the author of *Hands to Work: The Stories of Three Families Racing the Welfare Clock* (2002).

SUSAN JACOBY is the author of *Freethinkers: A History of American Secularism* (2004). She is a frequent contributor to the *New York Times*, *Washington Post*, and *Newsday* and has lived in New York City for more than thirty years.

DAN JANISON is the City Hall bureau chief at *Newsday*. He has reported for more than twenty-five years on local and state government and politics and has been a staff writer at the *Staten Island Advance*, the *Times Union* of Albany, and the *New York Post*. His work has been nominated for the Pulitzer Prize.

DAVID DYSSEGAARD KALLICK is a Senior Fellow at the Fiscal Policy Institute. His writings have been featured in *Utne Reader*, the *Nation*, *Newsday*, and the *New York Daily News*.

PAUL MOSES is an associate professor of journalism at Brooklyn College of the City University of New York and director of the Center for the Study of Brooklyn. He was formerly city editor and City Hall bureau chief at *Newsday* and was the lead writer on a team that won the 1992 Pulitzer Prize in spot news reporting for the paper's New York City edition. He also covered the Manhattan federal court beat for the Associated Press.

DEBBIE NATHAN writes extensively on social issues and law enforcement. She is co-author of *Satan's Silence: Ritual Abuse and the Making of a Modern Witch Hunt* (1995), and the author of *Women and Other Aliens: Essays from the U.S.-Mexico Border* (1991). She appeared in the documentary film *Capturing the Friedmans*.

JAMES A. PARROTT is chief economist and deputy director of the Fiscal Policy Institute, a nonprofit think tank focused on New York City and New York State fiscal matters.

HUGH PEARSON is the author of *When Harlem Nearly Killed King: The 1958 Stabbing of Dr. Martin Luther King Jr.* (2001); *Under the Knife: How a Wealthy Black Surgeon Wielded Power in the Jim Crow South* (2000); and *The Shadow of the Panther: Huey Newton and the Price of Black Power in America* (1994). He has worked for the *Wall Street Journal* and the *Village Voice*.

TOM ROBBINS is a staff writer at the *Village Voice*. He has reported on politics, organized crime, government, and labor in New York City for twenty-five years. His awards include the 2002 Investigative Reporters and Editors award for outstanding reporting, and the Association of Alternative Newsweeklies' award for investigative reporting in 2003. He has worked for the *New York Daily News*, the *New York Observer*, and *City Limits* magazine.

LUC SANTE's books include *Low Life: Lures and Snares of Old New York* (1991), *Evidence* (1992), and *The Factory of Facts* (1998). He is a regular contributor to the *New York Review of Books* and has written for many newspapers and magazines. He is the recipient of a Whiting Writer's Award, a Guggenheim Fellowship, an Award in Literature from the American Academy of Arts and Letters, and a Grammy for album notes. He teaches writing and the history of photography at Bard College.

RICHARD STEIER is the editor and columnist of the *Chief-Leader*, a Manhattan-based weekly newspaper that covers New York City government and unions. He worked from 1989 to 1993 as a City Hall reporter and labor columnist for the *New York Post*. He has written for such publications as the *New York Times*, *Philadelphia Inquirer*, and *New York Observer*. He is co-author of *The Odds Must Be Crazy* (1997).

Contributors

GLENN THRUSH covers Washington, D.C., for *Newsday*. He is a former editor of *City Limits* magazine, where he reported on housing and community development during the Giuliani era. He has written for the *New York Times* magazine, *New York*, the *New York Observer*, the *Village Voice*, *Spin*, and *American Demographics* and is an adjunct journalism professor at New York University's Science and Environmental Reporting graduate program.

MICHAEL TOMASKY is editor of the *American Prospect* magazine. From 1995 to 2003, he wrote "The City Politic" column for *New York* magazine, covering the Giuliani era. He is the author of *Left for Dead* (1996) and *Hillary's Turn* (2001).

Preface
Jimmy Breslin

ALWAYS I SHALL see him coming up Barclay Street with his flotilla of clerks, holding a small mask over his nose, walking to display heroism in a television studio, walking to become an illusion for his nation.

And also coming down the street were screaming fire engines, one, two, was there a third? Going past Giuliani to the smoke and flames and death.

They were going to the north tower—tower one—of the World Trade Center where they would die because their radios could not hear the police officers in the helicopters above telling them to get out of the burning building because it was coming down. The police might as well have shouted into the hot sky. The fire fighters could hear nothing, and the building fell on hundreds of them.

Giuliani went to almost all the funerals as a prestige mourner. Never once did he or any of those around him recognize that he and other politicians were a major cause of the deaths. There had been hearings about these fire radios in the City Council in 1999. Nothing came of it. The blood is all over the hands of the council and the mayor. Then the comptroller, Alan Hevesi, had a hearing on radios but few paid attention and again nothing happened. More bloody hands.

Giuliani named Bill Bratton the police commissioner. Bratton asked for a report on crime in the city. It was done by two working cops, Bill Gorta, a captain, and John Yohe, a sergeant, whose interest was computers. Their report started a system that was called Compstat. It identified the places where the crimes were and had the precinct commanders held accountable.

The crime was—what a shock!—almost all in poor neighborhoods. For the first time in the city's modern years, the non-white neighborhoods had law enforcement. This brought the crime down so far and so fast that people called this normal policing a miracle.

Right away, Giuliani walked to the center of the stage. It was occupied at the moment by Bratton, who was taking many bows. Too may bows. Giuliani kicked him off the stage. He was the mayor, and if things were going great then he demanded the credit. Which is only right in American politics.

The trouble is, Giuliani thought this made him Mussolini. In another life, as United States Attorney for New York, his office had put more Mafia bosses into prison than anybody before. Whether he was actually responsible for their imprisonment or the cases were compiled before he ever showed doesn't matter. Of course he didn't do that much. Of course he took all the credit. And of course he was entitled. He was the boss on duty.

He was a man who on the outside worked feverishly to control everything about him, even trying to govern the simple walking habits of the people. He turned out to be a desperately poor administrator. He had no feel for the city, which in turn never saw what was inside him. The inner person was blind, mean, and duplicitous. In the city's major problem, race, he was openly afraid of having people of color near him. He announced that he was the Keeper of Morals, and he tried to shut down an exhibit at the Brooklyn Museum. He also went up Fifth Avenue in a parade with his girlfriend. His wife and two children could watch at home.

His personal character is summed up by his using a judge, Lloyd McMahon, to write a letter getting him out of military service during the Vietnam War. And now the other day he is on television saying that a huge stockpile of missing explosives in Iraq is the fault of the army privates who were supposed to be guarding them. The election-year president is blameless. Get the privates!

I don't believe in luck. Luck is the residue of design. There was a Friday night when Michael Dowd, then a lawyer in Queens, came into the old Costello's on East Forty-fourth Street and had a bowl of clam chowder and talked to me about payoffs from Parking Violations Bureau collections to Donald Manes, the Queens borough president. Manes, who was extorting, would claim he was being bribed. Dowd had to tell his story first. The crime was in the Federal Eastern District. We had more confidence in Rudy Giuliani, who was over in Manhattan, but who would cheerfully accept such a complaint. So I wrote a column about it in the *New York Sunday Daily News*, where I was working and on Monday or Tuesday Dowd went to see Giuliani. Giuliani called me at the office and said, "Thanks." I said, "For what?" He said, "For the witness." It was the start of the biggest municipal corruption cases seen in many years.

Because he didn't know how to campaign, he lost his first try at mayor to David Dinkins. He won four years later.

In City Hall his inner man appeared, as the ogre it always was. He handled the enormous problem of race by a display of great nervousness if more than one black at a time entered City Hall. There was a day when Housing Works, an organization calling for housing for the poor, many of them AIDS sufferers, had a march on City Hall. They were a small band of the limping and weak, and they were shunted to a narrow space along Broadway.

Across the street, on the roof of City Hall, police had sniper rifles pointed at them.

*   *   *

Never in his time did Giuliani do anything but smile in a rich man's presence.

On January 23, 2000, at 4:00 a.m. on a freezing night, plainclothes cops with badges hanging from their necks stormed through the beds of sleeping homeless in the Fort Washington Armory on 168th Street and began pulling them out of bed, dazed and destitute, and putting handcuffs on them. They were being arrested for failing to appear in court in the distant past to answer for such heinous crimes as public urination, sleeping in the subway, and begging for food in public.

There were eighteen arrested in this armory, seven of whom were schizophrenics. At other shelters, another 111 homeless were arrested.

In City Hall Giuliani was bug-eyed and ecstatic. "These are quality of life crimes," he exulted. Not understanding for a moment that their crime was having no home while his crime was monstrous: torturing the poor.

Forever he shall be known for these and other acts against the weak of the city.

Introduction
Robert Polner

THREE MONTHS AFTER terrorists hijacked domestic commercial airplanes and piloted them into the World Trade Center, Rudy Giuliani presided at one of his final "town hall" meetings as New York City mayor, and it was not going too smoothly.

A long-time teacher stood up in the auditorium of a Bronx school to chastise the freshly anointed national hero about oversized classes, one of those perennial challenges to a good education that a flood of government black ink during the prosperous late nineties had failed to alleviate. Despite the mayor's history of blaming bureaucrats and unions, and his lofty rhetoric of reform, the teacher, a middle-aged woman, accused him of not knowing what was really going on in the schools.

You haven't been in the classrooms, she said, heedless of the growing signs of his agitation. You don't get it, she insisted.

For me, a reporter for *Newsday* who covered Giuliani's rise and fall as a prominent politician—and, because of September 11, 2001, his rise again—this charged-up moment was comforting because, finally, the mayor could be seen again in a familiar guise. Long before Barbara Walters dubbed him "America's Mayor" for his steady, and steadying, presence through the crisis of 9/11, many New Yorkers came to know him as I had—as a consistently divisive figure. In his inflexibility and peevishness, Giuliani could be his own worst enemy and the city's as well.

Even though the people in the Bronx school were made to feel somewhat uncomfortable, I had to smile. Giuliani was known for assailing his critics, sometimes evoking the late Senator Joe McCarthy by tagging their beliefs as "Marxist," airing the contents of sealed documents or leveling unsupported accusations. On this particular night, he accused the teacher of behaving like a "jerk." His tone was defensive as he labeled his questioner—rather than classroom crowding, uneven funding, or any of the myriad obstacles facing the nation's largest school system—as the type of individual responsible for the distressed state of the city's school system.

At the time, my memories of the terror attacks were vivid and my feelings raw. I'd watched the first flaming trade center tower crumble less than four blocks from where I gaped skyward. Now, at least, it seemed like old times again, listening to Giuliani's distinctive exasperation. And I breathed a bit easier. Notwithstanding his supposedly Churchillian aura, Giuliani was displaying his itchy, slightly paranoid core once again. And despite his lionization by the nation's media, underneath it all, Rudy was still Rudy—the same seething, complex, ultimately disappointing leader, spoiling for a fight.

* * *

I decided to organize and edit this collection of original essays by New York writers after leaving the City Hall beat in early 2002 to become an assistant city editor and later to take on a new beat. What spurred this project was my opinion that Giuliani didn't serve New York well, despite his admirable stewardship on 9/11, its darkest hours, and that September 11, 2001, has obscured many disturbing truths about his mayoralty. I suppose that this project was cathartic for me, but I was also motivated by my belief that people should know and remember the record of their leaders, especially politicians like Giuliani, who might one day aspire to the highest political office in the land.

In Giuliani's case, his exercises in self-promotion, exaggeration, and lashing out, which I witnessed over and again as a reporter, scarred an otherwise bountiful period in the city's life, the years before 9/11, adding up to a giant missed opportunity to improve life for most New Yorkers in many significant.

Though the mayor usually managed to place himself in the center of the city's story line-of-the-day—and had us think he was the source of all improvement—he was actually a spent force by the dawn of September 11, 2001. By that day, most New Yorkers had long since grown weary of the turmoil he created, his melodrama and solipsism, and began to focus on who would succeed him. He was adrift and heading to obscurity, a political ambulance chaser destined for irrelevancy and someone who would not be missed.

September 11, 2001, changed how Americans saw the world and New York's mayor. The waves of adulation were so overwhelming, they gave Giuliani the confidence—indeed, the hubris—to try to extend the last of his two allowable terms beyond the statutory two-term limit at the end of 2001. He believed that New York could not weather the immediate aftermath of the crisis without him poised at the helm. He was mistaken, though, and his attempt to broker this deal was heavily criticized and died a quick and unlamented death.

For me, one of the notable things about Giuliani throughout his tenure was his compulsive tendency to cause damage and overreach. His bid to overstay his last term of office was but one example. Given Giuliani's similar penchant for secrecy and paranoia, some critics compared him to another intelligent, suspicion-filled Republican—Richard Nixon. In some ways the comparison was apt. The waning days of his administration saw Giuliani removing the records of his mayoralty for secure storage in a private warehouse, including, at least by one account in the *Village Voice*, recordings of closed-door cabinet meetings and thousands of pages of official documents, memos, and keepsakes. I almost have to wonder if someday they will emerge for public airing without intermittent gaps. For now, though, much of this public record remains out of the reach of historians and journalists, of the citizenry, reflecting the mayor's awesome appetite to control future interpretations.

Unlike Nixon, though, it was Giuliani's open-to-view activities, rather than his behind-closed-door dealings, that accounted for so many of the more problematic aspects of his time in office. There was his continuation of hard-line policing long after crime had subsided, despite the widespread evidence of racial profiling by police and a tragic sequence of police shootings of unarmed black men. There were, too, his disproportionate cuts to the budgets of public institutions that most of the city's poor and working minority residents relied on, despite the deleterious effects; and there were his determined efforts to block the needy from receiving food stamps and other benefits to which the federal courts had deemed them legally entitled.

While it would be hard to imagine Richard Nixon walking a girlfriend home with news cameras whirring and flashing all around, Giuliani made the most of such attention after the *New York Post* exposed his alleged extramarital affair just as he was tooling up for a race against Hillary Rodham Clinton to succeed Daniel Patrick Moynihan in the United States Senate. Giuliani soon was diagnosed with prostate cancer and quit the race. He then floundered in what remained of his second term, and his once formidable political capital was all but exhausted.

The present day is a much different story, of course, and Giuliani stands flush with restored health, a hero's image, and the good graces of many in the Republican Party in Washington, whose delegates he welcomed with unblushing partisanship at its presidential nominating convention at Madison Square Garden in 2004. He could run for governor of New York. It is also conceivable he could seek the presidential nomination as early as 2008—something associates say he may do—and might again face Hillary Clinton in a race for the White House. This time around, divorced from his second wife and married to his third, he believes he will win.

* * *

From his very first days at City Hall, Giuliani impressed many New Yorkers, myself included, with a take-charge style, a tight grip on the details of the then–$32 billion city budget and his tireless work ethic. He raced around town in a white SUV, sirens blaring, a ubiquitous vehicle reporters soon dubbed "Mighty Whitey." The 24/7 crusader showed up day or night at the bedsides of injured policemen, the scenes of water main gushers, or shoulder-to-shoulder with snowplow drivers girding to battle winter's wrath.

With his instantly popular police sweeps of squeegee men, diplomat scofflaws, and sidewalk vendors of art, Giuliani built an effective case that an international city of 8 million could be steadied by one man's firm rule and, more significantly, could even be molded and governed. This was no modest feat of persuasion, considering New York had been in a great deal of trouble from crack, crime, and a national recession less than two years before he took office.

The trajectory of his mayoralty—his rise, fall, and rise again—began with a catchy promise that he would clear the slate of decades of Democratic-sponsored corruption and mismanagement. His election, he pledged, marked the start of a new order destined to transform a moribund bureaucracy into a center for merit-based hiring and bold action, a government reinvented. "We have a city to save," he declared. And one could understand why most New Yorkers harbored hope for improvement in the way the city was run and public services were delivered.

But observers who were willing to examine the City Hall–promoted storyline about a paragon of law, order, and civic virtue could already discern the seeds of Giuliani's eventual unraveling. The hints consisted of his early petulance, fixation on message control, and evident belief that the goal of stemming social disorder justified virtually any weapon he might deploy.

The first time Giuliani ran for mayor was in 1989; he lost to then–Manhattan borough president David Dinkins. Giuliani followed up in 1993 with a comeback victory by the slim margin of forty-five thousand votes over the incumbent. It was in these campaigns that Giuliani, a former Manhattan U.S. Attorney who had prosecuted municipal corruption in the late 1980s, demonstrated that he wasn't above gutter politics, smears, or expedient adjustments to his positions (as when he went from emphasizing his personal opposition to abortion during the 1989 Republican mayoral primary to vowing, during the general election phase in a heavily Democratic city, to uphold the legal right to abortion). Known for his rectitude as a former federal prosecutor and his outright disdain of partisan politics, he evolved on the way to City Hall into a full-fledged pol, and a truculent one at that.

After unseating Dinkins in 1993, Giuliani wasted no time running afoul of his professed standards of ethics and intolerance for business-as-usual. It wasn't enough for Giuliani to hire childhood friends and other close political allies as his key advisers. His insularity went much further. Despite his jeremiads about political patronage under Democrats, Giuliani went ahead and stocked the government all the way down to its least fashionable levels with patrons. And to help execute these personnel changes, he chose Tony Carbonetti, a twenty-five-year-old college dropout whose father, a friend to the mayor's late father, had already been given the post of director of the mayor's community assistance unit.

In the early months of that first term, agency commissioners were required to take dozens of City Hall referrals from the younger Carbonetti, perhaps even people apparently unqualified, unless they wanted their entire agency hiring budget frozen and their own jobs put at risk. Giuliani made it clear in many ways that he valued loyalty above all else and would brook no dissent or even, it seemed to some of his aides, constructive criticism. "A small man in search of a balcony," was how Jimmy Breslin described him in his newspaper column.

It became evident that Giuliani's activities in organizing his administration were beholden to his great fixation—message control. Though Dinkins had recruited a talented group of commissioners and encouraged a healthy degree of autonomy and innovation in the realm of policymaking, he developed a reputation in the local media for being less than commanding. Giuliani was determined never to be portrayed as Mayor Dinkins had been.

In addition to centralizing virtually all administration decision-making within the mayor's office, Giuliani kept close tabs on the city's traditionally independent department of investigation. This corruption watchdog agency had been made stronger as a consequence of the mid-eighties municipal bribery and kickback scandals involving crooked borough leaders and agency heads. Giuliani himself had prosecuted many of those cases as the U.S. Attorney in Manhattan. But as mayor he arguably compromised the investigation agency, an unfathomable act coming from a former gangbusting federal prosecutor. He hired a former colleague, Howard Wilson, to run the investigations unit, bringing Wilson to his 8:00 a.m. meetings to brief members of his cabinet on pending investigations. Giuliani wouldn't allow the department to have much autonomy, and summaries of completed investigations, public documents known as "closing memoranda," were no longer released.

Outsiders who sought such documents or other data upon which to gauge the reliability of Giuliani's claims about his administration's record encountered stalling, ostracism, or, at times, verbal abuse. Every City Hall steward has tried to manage the unruly New York media, but Giuliani went to much greater lengths than his predecessors to thwart inquiry, curb dissent, punish whistle blowers, and squelch debate.

New Yorkers shouldn't have been too surprised by the mayor's bullying. One of his more indicative performances actually came when he was a candidate for mayor in 1993. At a police union rally against Dinkins's support of legislation to create an independent, all-civilian board to review complaints of police brutality, hundreds of off-duty police officers, many swilling beer and waving posters that likened the black mayor to a washroom attendant, pumped their fists into the air as Giuliani shouted to them through a bullhorn. "Bullshit," the candidate cried in reference to Dinkins's proposal, and members of the excitable crowd roared with approval. Some overturned parked cars. Dozens soon swarmed across Broadway to City Hall, intent on entering the mayor's office. Detectives in plain clothes guarding the doors hastily locked the iron gates to keep out the mob and called for reinforcements.

Another sign of what kind of man Giuliani was and what kind of mayor he was to become was his quick dismantling of affirmative action programs in city contracting once he gained office. The belief that he was no friend of blacks was fueled over time by his selection of a nearly all-white circle of advisers. When a reporter from the *Daily News* sought racial breakdowns of the new administration, the journalist was quickly branded a "racial arsonist," a description he included in his story. Giuliani merely turned the untoward attention into another one of his indictments of what he liked to call "the old way of thinking," insisting that his maverick principles included a racially blind code for all decision-making. His much-underestimated tin ear didn't help endear him to blacks any more than his sanctimonious pronouncements about his "philoso-phy" of governance. When a reporter from the *Washington Post*, in 1997, asked him about his strikingly low poll ratings in minority communities, he suggested that blacks, first and foremost, should be grateful to be alive, given that the drop in crime had occurred to a large extent in low-income neighborhoods populated by minorities.

As much as statements like that seemed calculated to intimidate, settle scores, or reassure his base, they also reflected the character of someone surprisingly ill at ease with the normal give and take of pol-itics and policymaking—someone who loathed the kind of intellec-tual combat for which Ed Koch, another irascible mayor, will long be remembered. Giuliani gave few interviews except to those who could be counted on to suspend their disbelief or swallow his entire agenda. He used forums, such as his near daily press conferences, to denounce questioners like the reporter who, citing the mayor's own statistics, pointed to a drop in police visibility in neighborhoods out-side Manhattan. When the mayor was irked, he made it personal, as he did in this case, denouncing the perfectly logical question as ignorant. At other times he cut questioners short, changed the topic, or strode away from his podium in a huff.

New Yorkers, no wallflowers themselves, admired his willfulness, bluster, and iconoclastic image, though some were taken aback by his abrasiveness. He had a big-city persona after all, and if people were struck by the force of his personality, they felt he was being effective. He looked to many like the right man to run the city after a long and brutal recession. "New York City: We can kick your city's ass," was the slogan the brash new mayor chose to promote on "The David Letterman Show."

But as his temper and stridency became more familiar, he got under more and more people's skin. One of the traits he exhibited in his first term was a reluctance to share credit for the unexpected slide in the murder rate, even though the amelioration of violent crime predated his 1994 arrival and probably stemmed from factors such as the leveling off of the crack epidemic and Dinkins's approval of an income-tax increase to hire thousands more cops, which had nothing to do with Giuliani or his administration.

Giuliani coupled his hype with a stunning disregard for basic civil liberties. In scores of instances for which he will long be remembered, he denied civic groups their constitutional right to stage protests about his policies, only to be overturned by the courts time and again when the targets of these fiats appealed. The flow of adverse rulings led the mayor to denounce the judges who rendered them, including federal magistrates. He had little respect for the First Amendment rights of New York City's citizens and battled against free speech and the freedom of assembly with a mischievous and menacing fervor. In the end, it seemed as if he had no respect for anything or anybody he couldn't control.

He took a similar tack with two of his most talented commissioners. Ray Cortines was the independent-minded schools chancellor he inherited from Dinkins. After a barrage of insults, Giuliani calling him a "little victim" and "precious," Cortines resigned in 1994. This over-the-top ad hominem attack disturbed no one more than Ed Koch, who, despite his support for many of the mayor's programs, said he could never again speak well of Giuliani the person. Less than two years later, when Giuliani decided to dump his equally talented and independent police commissioner, Bill Bratton, Giuliani assigned his department of investigation to look into Bratton's on-the-job book deal as a possible conflict of interest. Nothing came of that, to nobody's surprise.

Giuliani had other issues. Though New York was shaking off the effects of the recession quicker than even Giuliani could have imagined, the city's deep-seated difficulties remained intact. New York City had one of the nation's worst housing shortages, a faltering public school system, unusually high rates of poverty, and was far too dependent on the stock market's wheel of fortune. These were problems that would never be resolved by a policeman's nightstick, hardline law enforcement, or insistence on civility; they were, in fact, problems the mayor wouldn't, or couldn't, even begin to address.

* * *

By the time Giuliani was ready to run for re-election in 1997, he was riding too high in the polls to acknowledge well-known vulnerabilities in the life of the city or discuss any second-term objectives at all. His campaign slogan was simply "Keep It Going!" And when, in the wake of his decisive victory over the Democratic candidate Ruth Messinger, he abruptly vowed to reach out to disaffected constituencies he said had not reaped the many benefits of his first term, his supporters burst into applause on election night. The press took note too, running stories for days that related Giuliani's Scrooge-like metamorphosis.

It took less than two months, however, before Giuliani returned to his old ways and telegraphed that his top priority was seeking higher office during his second term. He had worked hard in his first four years as the city continued to calm and began to prosper, shedding its threadbare overcoat for a corporate sheen. He'd refused during the re-election campaign to discuss whether he would actually complete his second term if elected. Now he made clear that he intended to use the second four years in office to try to hoist himself above and beyond New York City and to run for an unspecified statewide office.

So it was that Giuliani delivered his second inaugural address on a polar January 1, 1998, in front of a huge American flag. Not long after, he drove his anti-poverty prescriptions harder than ever and enlisted an enthusiastic Connecticut-born apostle of self sufficiency, Jason Turner, to "end welfare" in New York. The poor, declared the mayor, needed to be broken of their dependence on public assistance through the transformational power of work. No matter that the majority of welfare recipients cycled in and out of uncertain low-wage jobs, and on and off of welfare. Giuliani delivered bracing lectures on the importance of fostering the work ethic, while Turner, his social services commissioner, established policies designed to discourage the needy from applying for welfare and making sure they didn't stay for long. The strategy was called "Diversion." Under it, low-income New Yorkers and their children were sent by the thousands to churches, charities, unpaid workfare activities, or low-wage jobs in the private economy without any chance for training or education, reliable child care, or even—as a federal judge declared in 1999—the ability to exercise their legal right to apply for food stamps. In the Giuliani administration's view, any work was better than the addiction of welfare, even selling lemonade on a street corner, as the mayor once put it. Even as prosperity kissed many New Yorkers with money to invest in a surging Wall Street, the lines outside church pantries and soup kitchens and the demand for emergency shelter grew to historic levels. The city clearly became less accommodating of the poor, and many of those who gladly went to work for their assistance and sought to follow the inscrutable rules found themselves no better off and were often kicked off welfare for infractions like tardiness. Ironically, City Hall was at this time granting huge tax breaks and sometimes direct cash grants to any corporation or financial exchange that made an opportunistic threat to move its offices out of the city.

Starting in 1999, the "24-hour mayor" left town frequently to tout the reductions in the welfare rolls and the drop in crime and cultivate GOP support for his planned race against Hillary Clinton the following year. Most important to Giuliani was overcoming the discomfort many Republican leaders had about his 1994 endorsement of liberal icon Mario Cuomo, let alone Giuliani's positions in support of gun control, gay rights, and *Roe v. Wade*. After years of courting Democratic voters in city speeches, his out-of-town speeches often mocked New York City, stereotyping its citizenry as rude cab drivers, inveterate jaywalkers, and knee-jerk protesters, and painting a simplistic and inaccurate picture of a metropolis turned to self-reliance, public discipline, and economic success under his tough love.

Jetting back to City Hall between such addresses to conservative audiences, Giuliani tailored his few remaining administrative initiatives to his political aspirations, at one point proposing to change the line of succession in the city charter to prevent a Democratic rival, the city's Public Advocate Mark Green, from finishing out the mayor's term should Giuliani win the Senate race. At another politically convenient moment, the mayor famously went to court to penalize the Brooklyn Museum for exhibiting contemporary art he considered anti-Catholic (a bid for the large number of Catholic votes around the state). When the mayor's flimsy case disintegrated in the courts, he created a government committee to monitor art exhibitions in museums that received city funds. Civil libertarians mocked the blue-ribbon panel as an iron-fisted mayor's "decency committee," while another detractor, Bronx borough president Fernando Ferrer, described it to the *Times* as "something out of Berlin in the 1930s." The committee was soon ignored and then forgotten.

* * *

The pointless furor took place against a backdrop of growing local outrage over his administration's aggressive policing tactics. Giuliani, as rigid as ever, responded to waves of protests and acts of civil disobedience by notching *up* the pressure on street crime. He nearly tripled the size of the gung-ho, plainclothes Street Crime Unit, whose motto was "We Own the Night." Thousands of people, usually blacks and Latinos, were picked up for trumped-up misdemeanors and spent a night or two in jail before seeing a judge, only to be released for lack of evidence. While held they were checked for any outstanding warrants. Police strip searches became the norm, some fifty thousand in all, under practices the courts would later rule to be unconstitutional.

These unrestrained procedures had devastating effects for the social fabric that the mayor downplayed or ignored. Parents of minority teenagers in particular were filled with foreboding, aware that Giuliani would excuse virtually any type of police conduct. Some cautioned their children to keep their heads low and their mouths shut in the presence of a cop. Community organizers began visiting schools in Harlem and Brooklyn to advise black and Latino teenagers on nonviolent strategies to defuse potential flash points and misunderstandings when dealing with police officers.

It was little wonder, then, that many members of minority groups, as well as many whites, were quick to believe in early 1997 that the Brooklyn police officers who sexually brutalized Abner Louima in a Brooklyn stationhouse bathroom had taunted and threatened their now-famous prisoner into submission by telling him "It's Giuliani time." The account, initially from Louima's lawyers, was soon retracted, adding intrigue to the sensational case. The words had never been uttered. But the expression resonated among many as an unofficial, shorthand description of the era. It gained further force after Giuliani dismissed a series of recommendations from a $15 million task force he'd set up in the heat of the Louima episode to advise him on ways to improve relations between police and communities.

It was in March 1999 that another violent incident involving law enforcement crystallized the public concern about Giuliani's police tactics—the killing of Amadou Diallo, an African street vendor, by four white members of the Street Crime Unit. A slight man, Diallo was returning home from work at midnight as usual, entering the vestibule of the Bronx building on Wheeler Avenue where he shared an apartment with three roommates. The police officers saw him reach into his pocket. "Gun!" one of the cops shouted. But Diallo, it turned out, was not reaching for any weapon—it was his wallet, perhaps to pull out his ID. The cops loosed a fusillade at him, forty-one bullets in all, striking the unarmed Diallo nineteen times. He crumbled to the ground, dead at the age of twenty-two.

Word of the incident spread and public outrage was immediate. The Reverend Al Sharpton quickly organized daily demonstrations in which hundreds of black and white New Yorkers, including David Dinkins, performed civil disobedience in front of One Police Plaza, demanding that Giuliani acknowledge and halt racial profiling and police overkill. The size of each day's rally grew rather than dissipated with time. In one related demonstration, ten thousand people rallied on Wall Street one afternoon, with more than a few stockbrokers joining the unusual lunchtime protest.

Giuliani refused to revisit his policies, trotting out statistics to defend the police department, daily decrying "police bashers," and highlighting the occasional picket sign that likened the NYPD to the KKK. His aides, meanwhile, whispered to reporters that the mayor felt the local Democratic Party was being held in Sharpton's radical sway. But the public's anger overtook every attempt at City Hall—the building by now had been encircled with barricades and a tall gate, its front steps rendered off limits to press conferences or demonstrations—to discredit the dissidents or distract from their message. The situation got more inflamed when Giuliani flatly refused to meet with moderate black elected officials. But no one should have been surprised. He'd had little contact during his entire mayoralty with anyone who was not white, politically powerful, or in full and fawning accord with his policies. He was not about to change now, even as the feds began investigating his policies. State officials, particularly Governor George Pataki, seemed to go out of their way to undermine the mayor, out of rivalry, animus, or because they no longer saw any political advantage in associating with so polarizing a figure. Giuliani still needed state support to gain control of the city's international airports and school system and build a billion-dollar replacement stadium for the New York Yankees. But now the odds were running at least 100-to-1 against him.

It was a point of frustration for Giuliani, but it kept him from mismanaging the city's prosperity more than he had already while trying to advance costly pet projects and his political career. As it was, by 2000 he was well on his way to turning a $3 billion surplus (at its peak) into a $4.5 billion–plus deficit for his Republican successor, Michael Bloomberg, to grapple with—the worst flood of red ink in a generation.

* * *

In the spring of 2000, with his Senate race well under way and millions of dollars in contributions in hand from Americans who viewed his opponent, Hillary Clinton, as the devil's daughter—or wife—Giuliani was diagnosed with early-stage prostate cancer. As if that wasn't bad enough, he also made it known that he was separating from his wife of fourteen years, Donna Hanover—they had two children together—and had a girlfriend, Judith Nathan, whom he had been discreetly dating for some ten months. Hanover held a press conference of her own just outside Gracie Mansion to say she was being blindsided by her husband and promptly accused him of having had an earlier affair with his press secretary, which both he and the press secretary denied.

There would soon be another fatal police shooting of a black man, Patrick Dorismond, twenty-six, who had gotten upset when plainclothes cops conducting a sting in Midtown tried to "sell" him marijuana, and an officer's gun went off in the scuffle. The mayor's bungled response to the death of the Haitian-American security guard exceeded in sheer ineptitude his mishandling of the Diallo case. To broad and fierce outcry, Giuliani improperly released sealed records of the victim's juvenile court case from when he was thirteen years old, stating that he was no altar boy (though, quite literally, he had been one at the Brooklyn church he attended as a child). It may be difficult to imagine now, in the wake of 9/11, but at this point in Giuliani's career, he was beleaguered, and his once hard-driving administration was adrift. Suffering from the same disease that had killed his father, and his private life a mess, he finally declared at a packed press conference at City Hall that politics was no longer the most important thing in his life and dropped out of the Senate race.

Incredibly, it had all been for naught—the out-of-town barnstorming, the fruitful raising of funds, the political stunts, reversals and recriminations, his attack on the Brooklyn Museum. Hillary Clinton, of course, went on to defeat Giuliani's relatively little known understudy, a Long Island congressman favored by Governor Pataki.

* * *

With nowhere to go once his second term was up but back to being a lawyer, Giuliani tried, in what little time remained, to project a kinder, humbler face. He quietly retreated from many of the city's more objectionable policing practices, helping to put multiple federal investigations of racial profiling and other law enforcement problems to rest. He picked far fewer squabbles. And he registered newfound sympathy for the sick, citing his own recent experience with illness. He put every city agency to work signing up families for federally subsidized health insurance, though it was too late for him to have an effect. About 40 percent of city residents had no medical coverage, nearly twice the national average, but Giuliani had spent too many years ignoring, denying, or aggravating the problem. He'd once called on the New York State Legislature to reduce Medicaid funding and had grouped the federal medical insurance program for the poor with all the many forms of public assistance he felt fostered an unhealthy dependence on government.

As for the mayor's renewed promises to loosen up his style, to smile and show more appreciation for others, they proved far-fetched. Giuliani soon returned to entering public chambers warily, as if they were booby trapped, with his shoulders hunched under an expansive forehead and his gaze mistrustful whenever he detected the slightest hint of a challenge.

Running down the clock of his time in office, he merely went through the motions of being in charge, with daily cabinet meetings, occasional press conferences and his weekly call-in radio show. Rather lamely, he exhorted New Yorkers to venture out into the sunshine for their health, attend a parade, and root for his beloved Yankees. He increasingly disappeared into preoccupations, from his golf swing, to his acrimonious divorce case, to his life with Judith Nathan. What he would do after leaving City Hall, where he would live and work, had yet to be attended to.

Then, 9/11 happened, bringing a national crisis to his doorstep. And as a public official who was more comfortable with combat than with conciliation, he knew instinctively how to respond.

He was having breakfast at a hotel when the first plane hit and he headed downtown to his emergency command center. Soon he and his entourage were forced to flee from the facility, housed, oddly enough, at No. 7 World Trade Center near the site of the 1993 terrorism attack on the towers. The building collapsed about a half-hour after Giuliani, his aides, and his bodyguards had evacuated. He commandeered the nearest TV crew and took charge of consoling and cajoling a panicked public amid the scenes of horror.

For the rest of that cataclysmic day and the uncertain ones that followed, the mayor filled a leadership void as President George W. Bush and Vice President Dick Cheney were removed to undisclosed locations. Giuliani's front-and-center stewardship in the wake of terrorism won him support from even his most stubborn detractors and admiration all around the world.

The smoldering acreage of the former World Trade Center had not yet cooled and the death toll was still unknown as the mayor's political stock shot skyward. He received an honorary knighthood by the Queen of England, was solicited to address the United Nations, and was named "Person of the Year" by *Time* magazine. David Letterman sang his praises with unusual earnestness, and Oprah Winfrey welcomed him onto her set as "America's mayor." He was "Churchill in a Yankees cap," a *Washington Post* writer raved.

After leaving office, the first of two books he had been commissioned to write, *Leadership*, became a best seller. His speeches in turn earned him huge fees, his security-consulting firm, Giuliani Partners, racked up high-paying clients such as Nextel and Mexico City, and he became a regular on the national GOP rubber-chicken circuit. During the 2004 presidential race, he led the cheering squad for George W. Bush, and spoke stridently on the president's behalf at the Republican presidential convention. And in the glow of all the attention, his mayoralty came to be cast, inaccurately, as some kind of model of civic governance.

My purpose with this collection of original essays, each of them dealing with a different aspect of Giuliani's time in office, is to set the record straight before his next big political move.

1

9/10
Michael Tomasky

IT WAS THE sort of thing that became routine during the Giuliani years. A reading program for the public schools resulted in small lending libraries being sent to young children—kindergartners to third graders—in the city's elementary schools. Every book was stamped with the legend "Mayor's Classroom Library Initiative"—and in the Giuliani years, that first noun came to be so much more closely attached to the man than to the office of which he was the temporary occupant. It seemed as if every little project that emanated from the city's vast bureaucracies had to endure the mayor's personal and unforgiving review and be blessed with his imprimatur before making its way out to the citizenry. And so it came as a shock to some teachers and parents—at a school in liberal Park Slope, Brooklyn, no less—that a volume intended for third-graders, a poetry collection by Maya Angelou called I *Shall Not Be Moved*, included a poem that dealt with childhood incest.

The *New York Times* got wind of it, and it turned out that the "culprit" had been a secretary at some place called the Teachers College Writing and Reading Project, who had typed "I Shall Not Be Moved" into her computer instead of "We Shall Not Be Moved." The latter was the title of the intended volume, about a women's factory strike in 1909, by Joan Dash (not that Giuliani was a fan of strikes either, but they could be assumed to occupy slightly less objectionable ground than incest). So acute was the fear of the mayor's wrath on such subjects that Lucy Calkins, the director of the program, issued an unambiguous apology to the mayor and the schools chancellor in the *Times*'s editorial pages. It all might have bloomed into one of those inflammatory, bang-up, maddening controversies that Giuliani loved to place himself in the middle of. But it never happened. The *Times* story ran on September 11, 2001. The mayor might have been asked about it that afternoon at his normal press availability sometime around two o'clock in City Hall's Blue Room. But that, as we know, did not take place.

* * *

Giuliani went on to glory in the course of that day and the days that followed. All but his most implacable enemies were stunned by the grace with which he led the city through the attack. He was great. His reputation was burnished forever in those few days; he is one of those public figures of whom it can likely be said that we know already how the first paragraph of his *Times* obituary will read.

But what if 9/11 had never happened? What if the day had just ended as it started—a gorgeous, heaven-kissed, Indian summer day, whose sole tension reposed in the fact that New York City voters began the process of choosing Giuliani's successor? What, then, would Giuliani's reputation be? Who was the 9/10 Rudy?

It's worth recalling that New Yorkers were moving to take the city in a radically anti-Rudy direction that November. Yes, Giuliani still would have endorsed Michael Bloomberg, probably; and, probably, Bloomberg would have spent the same $75 million of his own money to win the election. But it was the relentless context of the terrorist attacks that put Bloomberg in office, the idea—advanced by Giuliani, and backed up in the city's tabloids—that neither Mark Green nor Fernando Ferrer, the two Democrats who were fighting for their party's nomination, could lead New York in the wake of the attacks. The "mere" threat of an uptick in crime under a watery, ineffectual Democrat would not have been enough to elect Bloomberg (who, after all, had no experience fighting crime himself). No, the most important credential for a post-9/11 mayor was not the ability to protect the city from peril, but to save it from economic collapse. The candidates' various recovery plans became central to their campaigns. It was in this area that Bloomberg's business experience came into play and helped vault him into office.

Without the attacks, a more complacent electorate would likely have reverted to form and elected a liberal Democrat. On the issue of crime, that liberal Democrat would have demonstrated a Rudy-like, and Rudy-lite, devotion to Zero Tolerance. But on most other questions, the city would have veered off into very un-Rudyish directions. Ferrer had proposed a tax for the purpose of funding after-school programs, and a heavily Democratic City Council would have given it to him. Green, Giuliani's chief nemesis during the years the latter was mayor, had promised education-related proposals that were the polar opposite of Giuliani's (education was one of Giuliani's signal failures). Both men would have cleared the commissions and the bureaucracies of the hundreds of Giuliani loyalists who have kept their jobs under Bloomberg. Assuming that the crime rate did not again climb, New Yorkers would have come to realize that life without Rudy was both possible and, if less entertaining, a bit more serene.

Giuliani was not, on 9/10, a beloved figure. At most, he was an appreciated figure. Virtually everyone recognized that he had, on some level, pulled New York back from the brink. Homicides had dropped by nearly three-quarters. In the city's most dangerous precincts, the decline had been on the order of 80 percent. The critics of the mayor's crime program tended to ignore these numbers and focus instead on the high-profile instances of brutality or questionable shootings (cases in which the mayor inevitably sided with the police). Those cases were real enough and worthy of attention. But the crime reduction was nothing short of astonishing, and it shouldn't be surprising that the city was grateful.

But gratitude is not love. It's not clear that New Yorkers—outside the *New York Post*, conservative Jews, and a few of the (shrinking) white-ethnic, outer-borough communities—ever really *loved* Giuliani. And that love was balanced by a lack of affection within the city's black and brown communities—and lack of affection is putting the matter mildly. New Yorkers had been given a chance to show their love by buying into various schemes Giuliani hatched to subvert a term-limit law that would have enabled him to run, in theory, until he died. But they never did. The people voted that two terms were enough. And when, in 1999, Giuliani tried to rig the terms of succession to the mayoralty, the voters emphatically rejected even that. So even in the best of times, love was conditional.

But it is fair to say that by late summer 2001, Giuliani had become the kind of partner from whom love is actively withheld. Complicated, hectoring, difficult, and churlish, he had made nearly everyone around him, by September 10, 2001, tired. Enough already. The Rudy of 2001 had become both a bore and a boor. Once you've called people "soft-headed Marxists who represent the old thinking" enough times, your point has been made. You grow tiresome.

The boorish part, actually, had come the year before—the public announcement of his separation from his wife before he had even bothered to tell her, the impact this act may have had on his children, and then walking his new girlfriend down Second Avenue with photographers trailing on the evening of, of all evenings for this man who had purported to represent a strict Catholic rectitude when it came to the moral shortcomings of others, Good Friday. Giuliani never got quite the spanking in the press he deserved—a liberal would surely have been denounced for lowering the city's standards of decency—although Donna Hanover, the estranged wife, did win the PR war, leaving the mayor a most unsympathetic figure.

After that episode, which preceded by a few days his withdrawal from the Senate race against Hillary Rodham Clinton, Giuliani retreated from the headlines and didn't generate much interest for a while. Hillary won the Senate seat easily, most political attention was riveted on the 2000 presidential standoff in Florida, and Rudy was far less appealing than the man New Yorkers had gotten to know in 1993. To be sure, the diagnosis of prostate cancer that came in the midst of all this gave the narrative arc a certain pathos it would have lacked otherwise. But the man did much to ensure that sympathy would not be his constituents' overriding emotion.

And the changes that overtook Giuliani in the final years of his mayoralty were not only personal. They were political. Giuliani had always been admirably independent of the national Republican Party. Call it a calculated necessity for a Republican mayor of a city with a five-to-one Democratic voter enrollment if you insist, but I think there was some sincerity mixed in with the strategizing. He was no conservative, in the national Republican sense. From his endorsement of Democrat Mario Cuomo over Republican George Pataki in 1994 to his frequent attempts to distance himself from the Newt Gingrich brigade, Giuliani had made national Republicans as painfully aware of his independent streak as he had the local liberal intelligentsia. But once the Senate race—and future presidential ambitions—appeared on his horizon, that, too, changed. Back in 1996, he had barely endorsed Bob Dole and had said of Bill Clinton that "most of [his] policies are very similar to most of mine." Before that, he'd supported Clinton's crime bill. By early 2001, though, Giuliani said Clinton was "the first president in a long time that hands America over weaker than he found it." This habit has only intensified in the post-mayoral years, culminating (as of this writing) in his speech at the Republican National Convention in New York in 2004, which included loutish attacks on John Kerry and a ridiculous assertion that Giuliani turned to his police commissioner, Bernard Kerik, at Ground Zero on the afternoon of 9/11 and said, "Thank God George Bush is our president." Anyone who knows Giuliani knows it is completely impossible that he said anything remotely like this.

* * *

Giuliani's crash-and-burn 2000 lowered the stakes on Giuliani-watching by a considerable degree. He opened 2001 by launching another in his series of attacks on the Port Authority of New York and New Jersey. Realizing he still had to govern a liberal city for one more year (and confident in the knowledge that national Republicans were no longer watching him closely now that he wasn't a Senate candidate), he proposed a final-year budget full of the sort of goodies made unserious by dint of their timing (a proposal to build a dozen new schools, a $600 million housing expansion plan). Studies revealed that in winter, the number of homeless families seeking space in the city's shelters had reached its highest point since the homeless epidemic of the 1980s. No one was quite sure what accounted for the new explosion, especially since Giuliani's policy had been to screen families far more aggressively than in the past.

But whatever the particulars of Giuliani's eighth year in office, the suspense of wondering how he would confront them was gone. He was used up. He had come into office in an explosion of activity. Barely a week after his first swearing in, a controversy at the Nation of Islam mosque in Harlem handed him the opportunity to tell the city that things would be different—no mollycoddling, no temporizing. There was a new roster of insiders for the city to get to know, mostly men who had been with him for years going back to his tenure as the U.S. attorney in Manhattan, like Peter Powers and Randy Mastro and Dennison Young; there was the bold new police commissioner, Bill Bratton, who unblushingly asserted his prerogative of nailing the bad guys by any conceivable means; and then there was Cristyne Lategano, communications director and alleged paramour (she always denied it), who joined his campaign as a twenty-eight-year-old with little Capitol Hill experience and who became, arguably, one of the three most powerful people in city government. Controversies arose during Giuliani's tenure with frequency. Not all of this was good. But it wasn't all bad either, and however one felt about the details, one could not escape the sense that we were involved in a turning point in municipal history and that the dialectic was moving forward.

But by 2001 it was all dead. His defenders in the media, who remained legion, took to writing columns saying that his task was finished, and he'd done everything he'd set out to accomplish. This was nonsense. There was the education failure noted above; no follow through on his promise to "reinvent" government; the budget skyrocketed during his tenure; and for all his tax cutting and talk of economic dynamism, he presided over a city economy that was generally flat during much of his mayoralty, at least before the tech boom. Others noted that all administrations lasting eight years (an accomplishment in itself these days) peter out and, by the final year, have already overdrawn the reservoir.

But it was clear to most other eyes that the mayor wasn't terribly interested in his job anymore. Giuliani had once been immersed in the minutia of municipal government. Sometime between his 1989 loss to and 1993 defeat of David Dinkins he and I had lunch, something it was then possible to do with the private-practice attorney who was recognized and waved at but drew few crowds. He told me, to my surprise, that he hadn't deserved to be elected mayor in 1989 because he hadn't known enough about the city and its agencies. So he'd spent the intervening years learning. By the time he got to Gracie Mansion, while it was often easy to take issue with his decisions, it was clear he'd done his homework. He seemed to know every small detail; through command of detail, he gained much authority.

But by mid-2000, fastidiousness had given way to demands for gigantism. The project he was working furiously to finish before he left the office—one that aides would have told you he was salivating to complete and announce—was to build new stadiums for the Mets and his worshiped Yankees. Each stadium was to cost around $800 million. The city's projected budget deficit for the following fiscal year stood at $3 billion. That's another thing people have utterly forgotten; blaming 9/11 for the city's economic difficulties became the standard, accepted line. But, in fact, the distress had existed before. Giuliani pressed ahead. News accounts of the period show put-upon state government officials griping (in background only; Giuliani's wrath was still considerable) that they were receiving an enormous amount of pressure from city officials to complete the deal before Giuliani left office. Governor George Pataki opposed the mayor's scheme, as did all six major mayoral candidates—the Republican ones, Bloomberg and Herman Badillo, did so politely.

And that's what it was going to be: the election of either his nemesis Mark Green or Fernando Ferrer, the ally of the mayor's other great nemesis, Al Sharpton. Yes, he would have been praised and celebrated as he left office, and in some respects most deservedly so. But an important part of his legacy would have consisted of the vast lost potential of a leader who did indeed have signal accomplishments but who would still have been leaving office with a third of the city loving him, a third hating him, and the other third just plain exhausted by him.

* * *

But, of course, 9/11 did happen, and today Giuliani's reputation, at least nationally, hangs almost wholly upon his performance responding to it. Time will tell whether the 9/11 Rudy will become subject to revisionism. For example, no one ever was quite rude enough to investigate, in the wake of the trauma, by what precise logic he decided to place the mayor's command bunker in the only building complex in the city (the World Trade Center) that had been the site of a previous terrorist attack (the 1993 bombing). That question may one day get answered in full. But until and unless that day arrives, the 9/11 Rudy will remain a national hero.

Meanwhile, it's worth remembering that the 9/10 Rudy existed, too. If he does someday seek the presidency, it's the 9/11 Rudy that will campaign, and it's the 9/11 Rudy—and the aspects of the pre-9/11 Rudy that fit the narrative, like the crime-buster theme—that most of the media will limn. The picture will be in some respects real, but in others, a flagrant distortion of a reality that, before 8:46 a.m. on that tragic morning, was far more complicated, fraught, and, to use a word that Giuliani himself would surely hate, mundane.

2

Prosecution
Jerry Capeci
and Tom Robbins

HE WAS THE nation's top mob buster. So it was perfectly okay for Rudy Giuliani to tour America doing stand-up imitations of Marlon Brando's Vito Corleone. His shoulders hunched and his jaw jutting out like the aging Don in "The Godfather," Giuliani got the marbles-in-the-mouth mumble down to a tee. "It's nice for all of *youse* to be here tonight," the shtick would begin. "You've come from many places. And now it's time to make the peace."

It was the perfect icebreaker for audiences, he said. He brushed aside complaints from spoilsport Italian-American officials who said the routine only reinforced negative stereotypes. He was the former United States attorney for the Southern District of New York, for crying out loud. He'd sent more big-time mobsters to prison than anyone else. So if anyone deserved a pass from the guardians of political correctness, it was he.

It makes for a great gig for the quintessential law-and-order Republican. Problem is, like many Giuliani boasts, the "I beat the mob" claim is vastly inflated.

The Mafia-busting moniker has always been a fundamental ingredient of the Giuliani resume. From 1983 to 1989, he was the leading federal prosecutor in New York's Southern District, the flagship office of the U.S. Department of Justice. On his watch, dozens of mafiosi were convicted of major crimes. No one would deny his accomplishments in that realm. But many people in the know, including current and former prosecutors, judges and defense lawyers, wince every time Giuliani claims credit either for "taking down the mob," or for hatching the plan to use the Racketeer Influenced Corrupt Organizations—RICO—statutes to do it.

Those are claims he makes loudly and often. In his 2002 book, *Leadership*, the ex-mayor put in writing a story he had told admiring journalists many times about how he came to use RICO against the mob.

"I dreamed up the tactic of using the Federal Racketeer Influenced and Corrupt Organizations Act," he wrote. "No one thought it could work," he added later in his book. The idea had come to him, he went on, as he was reading the autobiography of Joe Bonanno, one of New York's most venerable gangsters. "I realized that Bonanno's description of how the families were organized provided a roadmap of precisely what the RICO statute was designed to combat."

The way Giuliani used to tell the story, as repeated in the 2000 Wayne Barrett biography *Rudy!*, he was reading Bonanno's book at home at night when he turned to wife number two, Donna Hanover. "'Look at this,' Rudy said to Donna in amazement. 'This is a RICO enterprise.'"

Rudy Giuliani may well have had just such an epiphany. But so did several other people.

One of those people wasn't even a lawyer but he was in a unique position to recognize the threat posed by Bonanno's big mouth. Gambino crime family boss Paul Castellano—Big Paul to his loyal cadre—was the most powerful member of the Mafia Commission in the early 1980s and, as such, a prime target of law enforcement. The FBI, working with Giuliani's counterparts in Brooklyn in the Eastern District of New York, had succeeded in planting a bug in Castellano's palatial home on Staten Island. In 1983—the same year Giuliani became U.S. attorney—the Godfather was heard on the listening device talking about Bonanno's heretical book. The same light bulb illuminated Big Paul, and the shock of recognition was caught on tape. "They're gonna make us one big conspiracy," he was heard bemoaning.

On the other side of the law enforcement fence, the idea of making the mob "one big conspiracy" had been under discussion for years. Notre Dame University law professor G. Robert Blakey, a former rackets investigator and primary author of the RICO statutes, which were approved by Congress in 1970, spoke early and often about using them as a legal hammer against organized crime. By 1983, when Giuliani took over the Southern District, major mob racketeering cases were under way in Boston, Florida, Cleveland, and other places. The notion of using RICO against the Mafia Commission was alive in the Southern District prior to Giuliani's arrival.

According to John S. Martin, Giuliani's predecessor as the Southern District's U.S. attorney who later served as a federal district judge, the idea of a grand racketeering case, tying up New York's five crime families, was suggested to him by FBI officials in the early 1980s.

"I remember meeting with them [FBI agents], and they said they would like to put together a commission case through cases they had ongoing against each of the families," recalled Martin. "I think at the time I left the U.S. attorney's office we had at least three such cases under wiretap."

Those cases, against the Colombo, Gambino, and Bonanno crime families, were also pressed under the powerful RICO statutes, which allow prosecutors to use past bad acts, including murder, to compound conspiracy charges and tie together individuals involved in a joint enterprise. The Bonanno crime family case was based on the now-famous undercover mission of FBI agent Joe Pistone, played by actor Johnny Depp in the movie "Donnie Brasco." That case went to trial in 1982—a year before Giuliani took over—and resulted in convictions of four Bonanno family wiseguys. The prosecutors in that case went on to higher things: Barbara Jones became a federal judge in Manhattan; Louis Freeh was named a judge and then served as FBI director under President Clinton.

The Gambino case was aimed at a crew of murderous car thieves in Brooklyn who killed seventy-five people during a decade-long span of mayhem in the borough. Prosecutor Walter Mack, then the head of the organized crime unit in the Southern District, was ultimately able to indict Castellano himself in the case, charges for which the mob boss was standing trial when he was assassinated as he stepped from his limousine at Spark's Steak House in Midtown Manhattan in December 1985.

The Colombo case had started during Martin's reign and was also based on undercover work, in this instance a male and a female FBI agent posing as lovers aboard a luxurious yacht docked in Staten Island. Among the gangsters snared in the "loveboat" sting were many top guns of Colombo crime family boss Carmine "Junior" Persico.

Those cases were already well afoot when Giuliani took office. And other help came in the door shortly after he received the appointment. One of the most productive and ingenious penetrations of the Mafia's secret world came in 1982, when investigators for the New York State Organized Crime Task Force succeeded in planting a bug under the dashboard of a black Jaguar sports car belonging to Salvatore "The Golfer" Avellino, a millionaire captain in the Luchese crime family, who controlled virtually all of the private sanitation business on Long Island. Avellino frequently used the car to chauffeur his Mafia boss, Antonio "Tony Ducks" Corallo, who was also a Commission member. The bug was remarkably helpful and picked up Avellino and Corallo talking about the mob's interests in the carting trade, as well as the garment and construction industries. They were also heard talking about the Commission, the mob's secret superstructure since 1931.

The "Jaguar tapes," as they came to be known, yielded much solid information and spun off many juicy tidbits. But many cops and investigators with the local law enforcement agencies that were doing the grunt work—manning the bugs and wiretaps and following wiseguys around the metropolitan area—were hard-pressed to grasp the full sweep of the case.

Responsibility for explaining the case's significance fell to Ronald Goldstock, then the chief of the state's Organized Crime Task Force, who had to answer to members of the New York City, Nassau, and Suffolk county police departments and the Nassau County district attorney. Goldstock, along with his two top aides, Martin Marcus and Frank Rayano, held a meeting in 1982 on Long Island to try to get the participants to see the big picture of how all the elements in the disparate cases would ultimately fit together. In his pep talk, Goldstock told them the possibility existed of forging a bigger case than anyone had ever made. "Look," Goldstock told the investigators, "we're getting conversations about the Commission meetings. We might just be able to indict the members of the Commission."

But state authorities didn't yet have the RICO laws at their disposal. So Goldstock, Marcus, and Rayano went to see the new U.S. attorney. They even brought flipcharts to emphasize the different rackets shared by the Mafia Commission. Giuliani liked what he saw. "This is great," he told the investigators. "I'd love to do it."

There was one problem: many of the crimes fell under the jurisdiction of the U.S. attorney for the Eastern District, covering the boroughs of Brooklyn, Queens, and Long Island. "If you'll be on my side, we can do it," Giuliani said.

Snatching cases from different districts is a favorite sport among federal prosecutors in New York, and the weaker Eastern District, located just across the Brooklyn Bridge from the bigger Southern District, is more often than not the victim. In Giuliani's case, according to several people involved at the time, he wasted no time getting permission from allies in the Justice Department—where he had been working prior to coming to New York—to take over the cases he wanted.

Giuliani, who previously had been an associate attorney general in Washington for the Reagan administration, had clout and resources allocated especially to him by President Ronald Reagan's then–attorney general William French Smith. As a result of his inside connections at the Justice Department, Giuliani was able to big-foot the smaller jurisdiction across the river into letting his office use a significant part of the Colombo case, which had been put together by an undercover Internal Revenue Service agent. Giuliani's initial gambit to the Organized Crime Strike Force, which operated out of Brooklyn's Eastern District, was to conduct a joint investigation. Later, when the Manhattan aspect of the case floundered, according to former prosecutors who worked on it, Giuliani persuaded Smith to give him control of the entire case.

Giuliani had the Colombo case wrapped up and ready to be announced in the fall of 1984. The case featured Persico and several of his top lieutenants in a string of crimes. Among the lieutenants was Jackie DeRoss, a Colombo family member who doubled as leader of a corrupt restaurant workers union. Also included, much to the surprise of several prosecutors involved in the investigation, was the head of another union local that represented the city's hotel workers. Unlike the case against DeRoss, the evidence against union big Vito Pitta was shaky, Giuliani was told, and likely to result in acquittal. But the top prosecutor insisted. Including Pitta in the case would enable Giuliani to declare at a news conference that he had nailed the leaders of both unions who represented hotel and restaurant workers.

An announcement of the indictment—the first major mob case on Giuliani's watch—was delayed so that Attorney General Smith could come to New York City to join the Republican federal prosecutor at the press conference. The timing was politically favorable as well, since the press conference was held two weeks before the general election in which Smith's boss, Reagan, was seeking a second term. It didn't hurt that Pitta, the union official sandwiched into the case, was a big contributor and supporter of Democratic candidates. The charges against Pitta generated a second stream of stories as embarrassed Democratic politicians were queried about their ties to the indicted benefactor.

A year later, just as the case was going to trial, Giuliani agreed to sever Pitta from the other defendants after Pitta's lawyer argued persuasively that there was little evidence against his client. Shortly thereafter, Giuliani, without comment, quietly dropped charges against Pitta altogether. Unlike the indictment, which garnered headlines, the dismissal got almost no press.

The big case against the leaders of the five families finally came together in early 1985. Giuliani made multiple television appearances prior to the press conference. It was "a great day for law enforcement," he said, "but a bad day, probably the worst ever, for the Mafia." Giuliani had insisted he was going to try the case himself, but later handed it off to an assistant, Michael Chertoff, who won across-the-board convictions. (Chertoff became Secretary of the U.S. Department of Homeland Security in 2005.)

"Things always seemed to fall right for him," said one former top prosecutor who served contemporaneously with Giuliani. "When he came in, there were plenty of mob cases in the pipeline. He came in at the right time."

But not everything worked out exactly as planned. Among those convicted in the Commission case was a New York legend: cigar-smoking Anthony "Fat Tony" Salerno, who was charged as the boss of the Genovese crime family. Several years later, however, it emerged from mob informants that Salerno was nothing of the sort—he was a front for the real boss, a mumbling ex-prizefighter named Vincent Gigante from Greenwich Village.

The job of convicting Gigante, who claimed to be mentally incompetent, fell to the oft-neglected Eastern District where, without the hoopla of the Giuliani press media assault, prosecutors quietly carried out what many regard as the most significant mob cases of that era. At the top of the list was John "The Teflon Don" Gotti, the Gambino family boss who engineered the murder of his predecessor, Big Paul Castellano, and then replaced him.

The man who put away Gotti, the dapper, strutting gangster whose face appeared on the cover of *Time* magazine, was Andrew Maloney, who served as U.S. attorney for the Eastern District from 1986 to 1992. Although the conviction took place outside Giuliani's district three years after he had left his prosecutor post in March 1989 to run for mayor, many people still assumed that it was Giuliani who had engineered it. Maloney never blamed Giuliani for that. By 1992 the prosecutor-turned-politician had already developed a larger-than-life persona. Yet it must have rankled when, in the same year as the Gotti conviction, Maloney attended a conference of U.S. attorneys where, even among his peers, people came up to tell him what a good job Giuliani had done in taking down Gotti.

* * *

Connie Bruck, a writer, took a long, hard look at Giuliani's record as a prosecutor for *American Lawyer* magazine. Among the areas she questioned him about were the mob cases. In Giuliani's account, he had to go up against a hidebound, recalcitrant system to convince people to take on the mob.

"Prior to the victory in the Colombo case," he told Bruck in the piece, published in 1989, not long after he left the U.S. attorney's office, "there was a very different attitude toward organized crime.

There were questions about whether you could use the word Mafia, whether the Mafia existed, whether we could win a case like that—it was too big, too powerful, these people always got acquitted before."

The article prompted his predecessor, John Martin, to write Giuliani a private letter saying that his quotes in the story just didn't match the reality of the situation. Martin, then sitting on the federal bench, said he wasn't anxious to embarrass Giuliani so he didn't send it as a letter to the editor. Martin just wanted Giuliani to correct the public record the next time Giuliani was asked about it. He never did. For whatever reasons, the myth had captured the man, and he wasn't about to change the story, even if it didn't jibe with the facts.

"A long time thereafter, I got a letter from him saying that his claim was true," said Martin.

"He was a very bright and able guy, with a lot of able people working for him," said Martin. "But he did not invent the world."

3

Courtesy
Susan Jacoby

I FIRST SAW Rudolph W. Giuliani in person on a nippy December morning in 1993, as I passed the corner of York Avenue and Eighty-sixth Street on my way to buy a paper at my neighborhood news-stand. The mayor-elect, who lived at 444 East Eighty-sixth before his move into Gracie Mansion, was poking his finger at an ambulance attendant and asking, "Do you *know* who I am?" Meanwhile, paramedics were attending to a boy who had been hit by a taxi at the always-dangerous intersection.

Well, yes, the Emergency Medical Service lieutenant (I learned his rank from subsequent news reports) did know who Giuliani was. The EMS officer was trying to follow standard procedure and take the injured boy to the nearest trauma center—New York Hospital, only eighteen blocks away. But the boy's understandably distressed mother, who happened to live in Giuliani's building, wanted the ambulance to drive her son, in rush-hour traffic, to Columbia Presbyterian Hospital, some eighty blocks from the scene of the accident, because her husband was a doctor on staff there.

Giuliani leaped into the fray, calling the EMS worker an idiot and his stance "bureaucratic crap" (I heard those words, as well as various obscene epithets, although Giuliani later denied having uttered any vulgarities). The mayor-elect eventually succeeded in bullying the crew into acting against medical protocol and driving the injured youth to the more distant hospital. Fortunately, the boy only had a broken leg and suffered no ill effects from the longer trip. But it could have been otherwise, had he sustained a head or spinal-cord injury in which extra minutes can make the difference between life and death or between a full recovery and paralysis. That, of course, is why professional EMS crews—and New York's are recognized as among the best in the world—have standing orders to take injured patients to the nearest trauma center rather than a more distant hospital that family members might prefer.

After the incident, Giuliani portrayed himself as the defender of the average citizen in the face of an uncaring city bureaucracy. In fact, he was doing what he would continue to do best before he was transformed into St. Rudy by the tragedy of September 11, 2001— throwing his weight around on behalf of anyone he considered an ally. In this instance, in order to look like a big shot to his neighbor, he injected himself into a dispute that he was unqualified to assess.

Before that day, I did not have strong opinions about Giuliani, who was known to me mainly through a picture proudly displayed in the window of a neighborhood barbershop on York Avenue. But after I witnessed his manifestation of open contempt for a city worker clearly trying to live up to his lifesaving responsibilities, I could only think of Giuliani as Rudy the Rude, a schoolyard bully with a public podium.

* * *

Of all the myths that have sprung up around the mayoral tenure of Giuliani, the most baffling one to me is the notion that he was a champion of civility who turned New York into a kinder, gentler city. Part of that perception can surely be attributed to a significant drop in crime (a 44 percent drop in violent crimes during Giuliani's first term, from 1994 to 1998). But the falling crime rate was a nationwide urban phenomenon, not limited to New York, and has continued since Giuliani left office.

For many New Yorkers during the nineties, the dramatic reduction in the number of the homeless on the streets also contributed to the perception of New York as a more civilized city than it was during the financially strapped seventies and eighties. Both the falling crime rate and the disappearance of the visibly homeless probably had much more to do with the booming economy of the Clinton years than with anything Giuliani did. Giuliani's police force did roust the homeless out of their sleeping places with a determination never manifested by his predecessors. The mayor even took on the prominent Fifth Avenue Presbyterian Church, so unmindful of the sensibilities of rich, civilized New Yorkers that it allowed the homeless to sleep on its steps. In the closing weeks of Giuliani's administration, when the city was preoccupied with the aftermath of 9/11, he still found time to order police to move the homeless away from Fifth Avenue Presbyterian. If the NYPD's action made New York seem more civilized and "civil" to passersby on Fifth Avenue, it undoubtedly made the city seem less civil to the homeless themselves.

Giuliani always talked a good game about civility. "When we further the quality of life and advance New York City as a more civil society," he declared in a major 1998 speech, "when we constantly reinforce the fact that our actions affect one another, we'll realize together that inconsiderate behavior yields disorder and, more importantly, we'll realize the meaning of truly considerate behavior, which lifts the city up and brings us together every day."

Yet for all his crackdowns on symbols of disorder and disrespect—whether squeegee men, jaywalkers, or intrusive sidewalk vendors—the mayor seemed personally incapable of practicing what he preached. His post-9/11 sanctification has obscured the kind of irascibility, arrogance, and heavy-handedness witnessed by me and so many other New Yorkers.

*　*　*

A revealing moment in Giuliani's trajectory from hard-driving federal prosecutor to opportunistic politician was his participation in a hate-filled 1993 rally during his second mayoral campaign. (He'd lost his first race in 1989 to Harlem Democrat David Dinkins, the city's first and only African-American mayor.) An estimated ten thousand off-duty police officers, some carrying racist signs and many drinking beer, attacked Dinkins for his support of a civilian complaint review board. The out-of-control cops blocked the

Brooklyn Bridge; harassed motorists, reporters, and photographers; and trapped workers inside City Hall. Some of the racially charged anti-Dinkins signs read "Dump the Washroom Attendant" and portrayed Dinkins with large lips and an afro. Giuliani, a featured speaker, declared, to the applause of what amounted to a police mob, "The reason morale is so low is for one reason and one reason alone: David Dinkins."

Giuliani said not a word about the obnoxious behavior of his adoring audience (or about the racist signs and slogans). Police and their families were a key element in the coalition that elected Giuliani, and it is significant that he obtained their regard and their votes by his complicity in one of the ugliest, most uncivil demonstrations by civil servants that the city has ever seen.

From the start, Giuliani's actions and words sent a message to police that they would incur no penalties for treating ordinary citizens with an utter lack of respect. Early in Giuliani's first administration—I don't remember whether the year was 1994 or 1995—I was walking past the intersection of Seventy-ninth Street and Second Avenue during an Israeli Independence Day parade. Most of Seventy-ninth was closed to traffic, but a Chinese food deliveryman turned west anyway. The police officer at the intersection picked up a bullhorn and shouted, "Hey asshole." After a second "hey asshole" failed to halt the cyclist, he switched to "Hey fuckhead." Parents with children were visibly upset at the language—the deliveryman probably did not understand English—but no one confronted the policeman about his behavior. I was deeply unnerved by the whole incident. If cops feel free to shout obscenities through bullhorns in affluent white areas—where someone on the corner might actually *know* the mayor or the police commissioner—it is not difficult to imagine how they treat the poor and powerless on a regular basis.

Unfortunately, it was not only Giuliani's unquestioning support of offensive police tactics that made him the most uncivil mayor in the city's history. He was generally disdainful of democratic discourse and of those who held opposing views. The list of his targets is long and includes (in part): state and federal judges who opposed Giuliani's attempts to limit free speech, various artists and museums displaying art offensive to the mayor's sensibilities, critics in the press, any schools chancellor who disagreed with him, organizations serving the homeless and the poor, civil libertarians, the teachers union, community gardeners, and even those who did not share his passion for the New York Yankees—or for spending public money to promote various schemes of Giuliani's friend (and another paragon of civility), Yankees owner George Steinbrenner.

The irony was that I fully agreed (and still do) with Giuliani's oft-repeated contention that cracking down on relatively small violations of civic decorum is vital to improving the sense of well being of all New Yorkers. There ought to be zero tolerance for defacing the city with graffiti, urinating in public, invading privacy with noise, littering, and reckless bike riding on both streets and sidewalks. Had Giuliani announced a crackdown on passengers who insist on consuming smelly, sloppy food on subways and buses (one of the few forms of deviant but increasingly common behavior that he ignored), I would have applauded that too. And if it is impossible to catch every offender—as it obviously is in a city the size of New York—I have no objection to handing out hefty fines and making examples of the violators who can be caught.

The problem was that Giuliani's version of civility was always one-way—civility for me but not for thee. The deliveryman had an obligation not to ride his bike in a forbidden zone, but the police officer had no obligation to display ordinary courtesy to the miscreant messenger or to the neutral and innocent bystanders. Giuliani, who presented himself as a defender of the underdog, had one standard of civility for the people with whom he identified (his neighbors, police, or rich real estate developers) and another for those he considered alien—a group that included blacks, Hispanics, low-income tenants, and most city workers who were not police and firemen.

Giuliani's civility was never defined by the mutual courtesy that is the essence of genuinely civilized societies. For me, the enduring image of Rude Rudy's New York is one of barricades and barriers—on pedestrian crosswalks, at City Hall, and in Carl Schurz Park, where Gracie Mansion is located. Giuliani's largely successful effort to restrict public access to City Hall, long before 9/11, provided justification for increased security measures in all public buildings. His ugly concrete barricades were the physical embodiment of a civic philosophy that banned a New York tradition—protest demonstrations on the steps of City Hall.

Carl Schurz Park, which stretches along the East River from Eighty-eighth to Ninety-first Streets and is much beloved by neighborhood residents, was defaced for years by Rudy's concrete barricades. Apparently the mayor thought that protesters, thwarted by the ban on demonstrations at City Hall, might take the subway uptown and make a nuisance of themselves in front of his home. Every morning when I took a walk along the river, I had to step around those barricades in a park that had once been a tranquil oasis of green. There was also a police car, facing the river, outside the back of the mayor's residence. Giuliani was prepared for threats by land and by sea—even in the deceptively peaceful pre-9/11 era.

Giuliani's fortress mentality, which long antedated 9/11, may be one of the reasons why his impressive demeanor after the terrorist attack on the World Trade Center came so naturally. His idea of civility was always linked with a strong dose of paranoia, and in the wake of 9/11, paranoia seemed fully justified. Bring on the concrete barriers!

The current mayor of New York, Michael Bloomberg, is a much blander and less charismatic personality than his predecessor. New Yorkers may respect Bloomberg, but many do not like him as much as they liked Giuliani—particularly the memory of St. Rudy of the Twin Towers. I have my issues with Bloomberg too, but time can never erase one shining achievement, dating from the early weeks of his administration. The cement barricades disappeared from my much-loved park. At least one small part of the inhospitable and uncivil legacy of the Giuliani years has been vanquished.

4

Reputation
Jim Dwyer

ON THE EVENING of May 17, 1994, as the City Hall reporters for New York's major newspapers and broadcasters were wrapping up their work for the day, they began to receive phone calls from the mayor's press secretary, Cristyne Lategano. Heads up, she said. A big story was breaking.

The new administration—Rudolph Giuliani had come into office only five months earlier—had discovered a major scandal left behind by David Dinkins and his administration. It turned out that the city's Division of Youth Services, an agency that served as paymaster for community organizations receiving public funds, had overspent its budget by $11 million. In an act of subterfuge, contracts had been doled out without being registered—a violation of ordinary procedures. And most of that spending, Lategano and other City Hall aides told the reporters, had taken place in September and October of the previous year. As the story went, at the height of the campaign for mayor the Dinkins people had run the government gravy ladle at maximum power, sending buckets of money to suspicious "community organizations"—breaking the budget and bending the rules to do so.

The story got juicier. Lategano and another Giuliani aide revealed that within the past few days, they had discovered a crude attempt to destroy records at the Division of Youth Services. Someone entered one of the agency's offices and destroyed records on computer hard drives and other property. The only people with keys to the door were members of the agency's staff—led by Richard L. Murphy, the former commissioner, who had overseen all those mysterious contracts, and who left office with Dinkins.

The picture, as the mayor himself would say, was very disturbing: millions of dollars handed out by Murphy through some kind of backdoor operation and records destroyed in a Watergate-style operation.

By the time Lategano called with these tidbits, local political reporters were already past or bearing down on their deadlines for the next morning's papers. Even so, they moved quickly with her information. At the *New York Times*, the metro pages had already been laid out, but editors decided to pull a story from the first edition of the paper to make room for these developments from the mayor's office. The new story ran under a headline that read, "Youth Agency Overspent, Giuliani Officials Charge." Similar accounts appeared in the *New York Daily News* and *New York Post*. The story also made the 11 p.m. news broadcasts.

"My immediate goal is to get rid of the stealing, to get rid of the corruption, and to deliver better service to the children," Giuliani told the *News*.

With the leaks coming so late in the day, none of the papers or TV broadcasters managed to get a countervailing version of events from Dinkins or Murphy to include in the first stories.

Then, of course, life rumbled on. Scandals arrive and depart in New York City like subway trains, barely remembered beyond their transporting effect on the people directly involved. The sordid affair of the Division of Youth Services would, however, have a round trip. After the splatter from the original stories dried, reporters tracked down Dinkins and Murphy and dutifully relayed their responses that they had done nothing wrong. One or two of the follow-ups even mentioned that Murphy had an impeccable reputation in the social services field in New York

New York Newsday reporters Michael Powell, Nick Chiles, and Bob Liff and *Times* reporter Jonathan Hicks found holes in the Giuliani indictment, but at that point, the whole matter was turned over to the city's Department of Investigation—an agency controlled by Giuliani. For good measure, the city comptroller's office also got involved.

Not quite a year later, in March 1995, the results of the investigations finally came out. No contracts had been awarded to help the Dinkins campaign. It turned out that there had been no excess spending. In fact, the city comptroller established that the Division of Youth Services under Murphy had actually underspent its budget by a few million dollars.

And the break-in and destruction of computer records? The ten-month investigation established that a clock radio and television might have been stolen, though even that was not entirely certain. Other than that, nothing had vanished or been vandalized. No records. No hard drives. Not a byte was out of place.

If nothing was amiss, where had all the tales of scheming, stealing, and skullduggery come from? It is not hard to imagine how some of the confusion arose. Indeed, Murphy had awarded more contracts than he had money for—but he knew from experience that at least some of the groups would not be able to carry them out, so that in the end, he would be on target to meet his budget. He was right. As for the destroyed disk drives, someone apparently had difficulty turning on a computer, and this unremarkable event, combined with a door that had been left unlocked, was turned into a black-bag operation of gravely sinister aspect.

Asked about the false charges he and his assistants had spread, Giuliani shrugged. "That happens all the time, and you write stories about those things all the time," he said. "Sometimes they turn out to be true. And sometimes they turn out to be wrong."

Allegations happen, the mayor was saying, and he was right. Yet given the gravity of the charges that were being made by Giuliani, perhaps the lesson was this: spend a few hours checking out the facts before going public. This would have spared the reputations of David Dinkins, his vanquished predecessor, and Richard Murphy, the alleged ringleader of the nonexistent scandal. But other matters of state were at hand, more urgent than someone else's good name.

At the very time that the story came out, the New York papers had been covering Giuliani's own appointments at the Division of Youth Services. His first commissioner was a minister who turned out to have serious tax delinquencies. Moreover, Giuliani was larding the agency with patronage employees with no particular expertise in youth services—one was an airline mechanic—but who had been diligent in their service to his election campaign.

In fact, on the night that the Giuliani people were pushing the story of the missing money and records, the *Times* had a story set in type on Giuliani's use of the agency as a political dumping ground. That story—which turned out to be true—was the one that the editors pulled to make space for Giuliani's alternative account, a smear that turned out to be false, down to the last malignant iota.

To those who first came to appreciate the former New York mayor in recent years—in the era of Giuliani Transcendent, aglow in his exemplary post-9/11 deportment—it may come as something of a surprise that political slime operations were standard operating procedure in the eight years that he ran City Hall.

From its earliest days, the Giuliani administration was famously tireless in shaping public discussion and image of the mayor and other figures who wandered within radar range of the news media. Sometimes, the mayor and his aides dragged people like Richard Murphy by the scruff of their necks to make sure they got into range. In the beginning, Giuliani's enthusiasm for his own image was taken as his due, the garden-variety narcissism typical of many powerful people. What came as a surprise, at least initially, were his fondness for filleting the reputation of others, his ability to conjure the unworthiest qualities in someone he saw as a political opponent or threat, and his regular discovery that even the mildest critic was someone who could serve as darkness to his light—in sum, his absolute genius at finding mirror opposite images for his generous self-regard.

* * *

For those who might think the example of Richard Murphy was an aberration, the folly of an inexperienced administration, the case of James Schillaci warrants study. To begin with, it had almost nothing to do with the political operations of City Hall. Schillaci was just a citizen with a reasonable grievance.

One morning in May 1997, Schillaci was driving east on Fordham Road in the Bronx, passing the long fence of the Bronx Zoo. Cars on that stretch of road often pick up a decent head of steam—by New York standards, at least—because there are no traffic signals for about a quarter mile, except for a single blinking orange light. The orange light was set up outside a little-used driveway that served the zoo. And of course, it was there to urge caution, not to stop traffic.

As Schillaci drove past the zoo, the signal switched from blinking orange to a steady red. Schillaci, practically on top of the light when it turned red, blew right past it. In the next instant, a police car pulled out of the driveway. Schillaci was nailed with a summons for $125.

A limousine driver and native of the Bronx, Schillaci frequently drove that stretch of road and had never seen that light turn red before. He suspected that he had wandered into a small-town speed trap that somehow had been plunked down next to the zoo. The matter, he decided, bore further investigation.

Some days later, he returned to the spot and watched. Sure enough, a pair of cops were parked in the zoo driveway, back from the road. A few times, the patrol car crept forward, then rolled backwards, as if the police officers inside were peeking onto the road. It did not take long before they found people like Schillaci, running the red light. But how had they turned the blinking orange light to red? It seemed to go on every time they crept forward.

The answer, Schillaci observed, was in the driveway, where a pressure plate served as a switch. Because so few vehicles used that driveway to leave the zoo, there was no need for regular traffic control. But the weight of the car sent a signal to the blinking orange light, turning it red, eventually stopping traffic, and making it possible for a vehicle to exit that driveway. Using their patrol car, the police officers were turning the light red, then catching the drivers who almost never encountered anything but a blinking orange.

For his little surveillance operation, Schillaci had brought along a videotape camera and recorded the officers as they issued ticket after ticket to people who shot through the red light just as he had. With evidence in hand, he called the Civilian Complaint Review

Board. They referred him to the chief of department. That office passed him to the police transportation division. From there, he was directed to the Traffic Investigation Unit. Those officers referred him to the Internal Affairs Division. But that unit said it was a matter for the Bronx Borough Command.

On August 8, he took his complaints to Rudolph Giuliani himself, calling the mayor's radio talk show and telling him about the red-light trap. The mayor said he would have someone look into it. Schillaci gave his information to a call screener. The police quickly decided that its officers had broken no laws.

Having wandered like a mouse in a maze, Schillaci brought his videotape to public advocate Mark Green, an eternal nemesis of Giuliani. In short order, Green delivered Schillaci to the *Daily News*. The story of the "traffic signal switcheroo" ended up on page one of the August 26, 1997, paper.

At noon that day, Schillaci answered the door of his home and found two sergeants looking for him. They had a warrant for his arrest. Somewhere, a record had turned up that showed he had not paid two traffic tickets from 1984. Now, on the very day he complained in public about a police red-light trap, he found sergeants at his door, eager to address a thirteen-year-old infraction.

They put him in handcuffs.

"Isn't there a statute of limitations on this?" Schillaci asked.

"If you committed murder, we could go after you forever," he remembered one of the sergeants saying.

These were old traffic tickets, though, not murder. Later that day, when Schillaci was brought in front of a judge, he did not have a chance to open his mouth before the judge spoke. "Dismissed," he said.

"I was walking out the door before the two cops who arrested me got out of their seats," Schillaci recalled.

The city was not through with him. The arrest on the old tickets had set off another wave of stories, none of them flattering to the police department. The next day, the mayor's press secretary called an editor at the *Daily News* and portrayed Schillaci as a career criminal with a long rap sheet. Her suggestion was that a reporter should ask about it. So a reporter was assigned to ask about the rap sheet of James

Schillaci. Not surprisingly, the chief spokeswoman for the police commissioner just happened to have it handy when asked.

She read off a list of convictions—bad credit cards, burglary, sodomy—that were pretty serious. At a press conference, the mayor waited for the first question about Schillaci, then launched into an attack on him, the press, and anyone who believed their stories. He waved the rap sheet in front of the cameras. He accused the journalists of "police bashing" for reporting Schillaci's account of the red-light trap. They were taking the word of a disgraceful career criminal over the police officers who put their lives on the line every day.

There was one problem. While Schillaci did have a record for credit card fraud—it was nearly twenty years old—the sodomy and burglary charges, which also were nearly twenty years old, had been dropped after his arrest. They turned out to be the residue of an unhappy breakup with a girlfriend, and prosecutors never even put them before a grand jury. And even if he had been convicted of the Lindbergh baby kidnapping, Schillaci had a videotape that proved he was telling the truth about the red-light trap. Schillaci's mother called for Giuliani to retract his claim that her son was a convicted sodomist.

The mayor scoffed. "There is nothing to apologize for," Giuliani said.

Schillaci sued. Giuliani scoffed again. He said that writers at the *Daily News* had developed "a romantic attachment" to Schillaci and were ignoring the facts. After Giuliani left office, the city paid $290,000 to settle Schillaci's case. "What was he doing? He wasn't urging the overthrow of the government," said Michael Spiegel, the attorney for Schillaci. "He was complaining about a red light. And they pulled out the howitzers."

* * *

Asked once about his habit of taking what were, by New York standards, extreme positions, Giuliani launched into an exposition of his theories on government reform. In order to move the dead weight of the status quo even an inch, you had to set dramatic, perhaps unreachable goals. Nothing about his extremism was irrational; it was all, he explained, a carefully honed and logical approach to a world mired in old and unproductive ways of doing things.

Yet his attacks on individuals often seemed as much a product of temperament and impulse as any tactical forethought.

One winter night, a man named Patrick Dorismond walked out of a bar near the Port Authority bus terminal and was approached by an undercover cop seeking a drug deal. Dorismond angrily rebuffed the officer. A scuffle broke out, and Dorismond was shot dead. He was twenty-six. The death of Dorismond—not long after the shooting of Amadou Diallo, twenty-two, killed by undercover officers as he stood in the doorway of his own building, holding a wallet—created enormous tensions for Giuliani. Nothing negative could be said about Diallo, who appeared to have no criminal record of any kind; indeed, after he was shot, police officers went into his apartment and upended his room, pulling curtains off the windows and emptying drawers. What they were searching for was never clear, but it is a safe bet that if Diallo had secreted a marijuana cigarette, crack pipe, or gun in his room, he would have been portrayed not as an unarmed man at whom police officers had fired forty-one shots, but as a shady, violence-prone figure involved in the drug trade. (The search, the mayor said, was part of the "normal, investigative things" done in such cases.)

Dorismond, on the other hand, did have a juvenile criminal record—all of it from more than a decade in the past, when he was thirteen. In theory, juvenile criminal records are sealed. Their relevance to an episode more than a decade later was debatable. But just as the police officer who shot Dorismond was issuing a statement of regret and condolences to the family, Giuliani made his juvenile rap sheet public.

"I would not want a picture presented of an altar boy, when in fact maybe it isn't an altar boy," he said.

A few days later, a television newsman from *New York 1 News*, Dominic Carter, had a memorable exchange with the mayor.

Q. He was an altar boy, in fact. On reflection, do you regret not going to see the Dorismond family?

A. *I think that's not a correct juxtaposition of statements, nor intended for any, any kind of decent or useful purpose.*

Q. *Why not? You said he was [not] an altar boy?*

A. *Let's not, let's not, let's not get into a dispute over it. I don't desire to do that.*

Q. *But, Mr. Mayor . . .*

A. *Next question, please.*

Q. *Mr. Mayor, it's a legitimate question.*

A. *No, no.*

Q. *Either he was an altar boy, or he wasn't.*

A. *The question wasn't . . .*

Q. *His mother says he was.*

A. *I'm not going to get into an intellectual parsing of that question. That is not a fair question.*

Q. *[Garbled]*

A. *The question is intended, the question is intended to create a dispute, not to elicit intelligent information.*

Q. *Do you not owe an apology to the family?*

A. *As I said, the question was intended to create a dispute. It's an argumentative question. It doesn't really mean what it says. And I'm not going to answer in that fashion.*

* * *

Perhaps the mayor's temper when it came to the shortcomings of other people really was just another wrench or screwdriver in the toolbox of political reform. Still, it was hard to understand at times.

At 2:00 a.m. on the coldest night of the winter of 2000, the police raided several homeless shelters across the city. They arrested 149 people on outstanding warrants. Virtually all of the warrants were for offenses below misdemeanors, such as drinking on the street, urinating in a subway tunnel, and so forth. And many of them were seven or eight years old. Most of those arrested had afflictions, such as mental illness and substance abuse, common to those who end up on the street. A good number were pulled out of small shelters that had been set up precisely to make sure they were taking their psychiatric medicines and to keep at least a modicum of regularity in their lives. When an article by *New York Times* reporter Nina Bernstein recounted the arrests, the mayor exploded.

"There's no immunity in the law that says if you are homeless, you then get away with committing a crime," Giuliani said. "You can ignore the problem and say, 'Gee, I'm such a big, fuzzy-headed liberal that I'm going to walk away from it.' That's New York in the 1980s. That's New York City with 2,000 murders."

This was zero tolerance of crime, he explained. People needed to understand that was how he had made New York safe. Even these pitiful individuals, with their pathetic offenses against public order, warranted simultaneous raids on the coldest night of the year to drag them from their beds. They were a potentially lethal threat to hundreds or thousands of people.

It is dangerous for anyone to speculate on what is truly inside the head of another person, yet Giuliani compulsively disclosed his state of mind, and often enough, it seemed to be a state of rage. Why and how this should be so is beyond guessing. Only toward the end of his second term as mayor did a biography called *Rudy!*, by Wayne Barrett, the investigative journalist for the *Village Voice*, reveal that during the Great Depression Giuliani's own father, Harold Giuliani, had robbed a milkman at gunpoint on the Upper East Side of Manhattan. He was sent to prison, then paroled, just in time for his wedding. All this was long before Harold Giuliani's only child was born, and that son responded to the revelation by saying that he did not know anything about the matter.

There was, however, another case involving Harold that Rudolph Giuliani surely was aware of. As a teenager, Giuliani was with his father during a peculiar episode in a park restroom that resulted in Harold's arrest for loitering. The charge was dismissed, but the episode took an emotional toll on Harold, according to Barrett.

"The influence my father had on me was to drill into my skull from the time I was a little boy that you had to be very honest," the mayor said of his father. It is plain that Giuliani loves the memory of Harold Giuliani, but life with father did not seem to burden the future mayor with much empathy.

When the police physically ripped mentally ill homeless men out of their beds for unpaid summonses of the sort that Harold Giuliani once was served with, the mayor could not have seemed more eager to publicly endorse the raids and to portray these men as potential murderers. Yet with a bad turn of luck, one of those men jailed for public drinking or urination might have been Harold Giuliani.

It hardly seemed to matter. The homeless could just get in line behind the ousted public servants, the whistleblowers, the dead citizens. For so many of the wounded, the Giuliani City Hall had a fresh supply of mud handy. Failing that, there was always salt.

First Person

Rosalie Harman

ROSALIE HARMAN WAS *a veteran social worker for the city's child protective service when she was suspended for thirty days by the Giuliani administration for speaking to the media after the death of six-year-old Elisa Izquierdo. Elisa's case was gruesome and tragic, and it drew an enormous amount of attention after it was revealed that the child welfare agency had gotten numerous reports about her mistreatment prior to her fatal beating, allegedly at the hands of her mother. Harman, for her part, felt she had been improperly punished for discussing the much-troubled service with a reporter for ABC's* World News Tonight. *The New York Civil Liberties Union agreed with her and sued the city on her behalf in 1996, one of dozens of First Amendment suits prompted by the Giuliani administration's clampdown practices. She won at the first level, the city appealed, and in 1998, a federal appeals court panel held that the city's policy of requiring employees to obtain permission to speak to the media was a violation of free speech. Harman settled with the city for $12,000, the value of pay and benefits lost in her suspension. She gained a reassignment at less pay and then retired "with a certain amount of bitterness."*

"It was a very deep thing, very deep for me. I was working twenty-three years for child welfare and was in the homemaking unit, which trained mothers in how to deal with stress and with the family.

Giuliani came through with a policy of budget cutting, and I got very upset. I remember there was a client at the time who had lupus, she was seriously ill. They said, well, we have to cut the service because it's a 'chronic condition.' I told my director, listen, the woman has a disease that's not going to get better, and she needs this help.

I'm usually a quiet person. I don't make a fuss. But I was furious. I went to the public advocate and told them I was concerned about these budget cuts and felt something terrible was coming down the road. And what happened? Elisa Izquierdo happened. It was just one of many cases of this kind, but very high profile.

My agency began questioning any employee who had ever dealt with this family. One was a person from my unit who had seen Elisa when she was a baby. They questioned her like she was a criminal and she came out crying. She had nothing to do with what happened to the child. She was a good worker—I had supervised her and she was good.

So I called the public advocate again and they asked me, Do you want to go on television? I did, on my lunch hour, not far from my office. The interviewer, she thanked me and said I was very brave for doing this. I thought, What does she mean by that?

I worked six more weeks and nobody said a word. Then the managers and the directors—they were political appointees, you know, and wanted to get ahead—had me suspended for 'violating confidentiality rules.' It was a technicality. But their attitude was 'Kill the messenger.'

I did my thirty-day suspension, and asked Norman Siegel of the New York Civil Liberties Union to escort me to work on my first day back. I was such a wreck. I had sharp stomach pains. Right away, the director of my Brooklyn Field Office sent word that Mr. Siegel was not allowed upstairs, so I went up to her office by myself and when she opened the door it was like she was seeing a ghost. She screamed and she slammed the door shut, then reopened it, with trepidation. Why was I such a threat? I believe that she felt I could be a danger to her job under Giuliani.

After that, every effort, I felt, was made to find fault with my work, and I eventually realized I had to leave child welfare.

Giuliani, he probably wouldn't know my name. But I think of him as The Great Enforcer. I can't think of him as a villain; I mean, he loves opera, and so do I. But on civil liberties he was horrid, horrid, horrid."

5

Need
Neil deMause

"By the year 2000, New York will be the first city in the nation, on its own, to end welfare." —Rudolph Giuliani, July 1998

WHEN RUDY GIULIANI took over City Hall in 1994, 1.1 million New Yorkers—more than one in every eight—were getting some form of public assistance. Eight years later, the total stood at a little more than half a million. As columnist John Corry wrote triumphantly in the conservative *American Spectator*, "New York was the poster city for liberalism gone sour. But under Giuliani the Zeitgeist now has changed."

It was undeniably an impressive statistic. In his two terms of office, Giuliani rolled back the city's welfare rolls to where they had stood in the mid-1960s, at the very dawn of Lyndon Johnson's War on Poverty. By moving six hundred thousand New Yorkers off the rolls—more people, the mayor liked to point out, than the population of Buffalo—the city was doing its part to create a new social contract that would move poor people from dependency on government handouts to self-sufficiency. "The city gives more help than any city in America presently does and will continue to do that," Giuliani said shortly after taking office. "The city is going to be asking for something in return for giving that help."

They were inspiring words. If only any of them had been true.

* * *

Rudy Giuliani was hardly the only American politician to declare war on welfare. The same year Giuliani took office, Newt Gingrich made "welfare reform" one of the planks in his Contract With America, the only one, it turned out, that would end up signed into law by President Bill Clinton. Giuliani, though, got there first, and his reforms would have a somewhat different focus. While the federal welfare law contained much talk of encouraging marriage and battling illegitimacy, City Hall's rhetoric and prescriptions were almost exclusively concentrated on work. "If you're an able-bodied young person," wrote Deputy Mayor John Dyson, "the taxpayers of New York City are not going to pay you to stay home. Go to work. If you don't want *our* jobs, go out and get your own."

"Our" jobs would, at first, consist largely of workfare assignments—twenty-plus hours a week picking up trash or answering phones for city agencies, in exchange for a "wage" equivalent to a monthly welfare check. Giuliani portrayed his Work, Accountability, You—WAY—as a descendant of Franklin D. Roosevelt's Works Progress Administration. Critics labeled it "slavefare," pointing out that WAY workers were paid barely minimum wage and were not offered the right to sick days, health benefits, or protections from sexual harassment or capricious dismissal.

If the largest workfare system in the nation was the public face of Giuliani's welfare policy, WAY served a very different purpose in practice: purging the rolls of anyone the administration deemed unworthy of assistance. Early in his second year in office, Giuliani announced that, thanks to what he termed "fraud detection," more than 10,000 applicants to the Home Relief program for single adults had been rejected, a figure he called "close to astounding." Governor George Pataki, standing at his side, proclaimed the development "an extraordinary success."

Heather Mac Donald of the Manhattan Institute, the conservative and pro-Giuliani think tank founded by William Casey before he went on to head Ronald Reagan's CIA, would later write: "Did people leave the rolls in droves? Yes—because many people decided that if asked to do anything for their welfare check, look for a job, say, they would rather not bother."

Yet to those who took the time to talk with soup kitchen operators and Legal Aid attorneys, there was a simpler and far more worrisome explanation for the success that WAY was having in thinning out the welfare rolls. Liz Krueger, who was then associate director of the Community Food Resource Center and the mayor's most persistent welfare-policy critic, put it this way: "If you're the government, it's really easy to keep people off welfare. You don't need a lot of tricks up your sleeve. You're the one standing by the front door, and you just lock it."

Within the Giuliani administration, the preferred term for the purging process was "diversion." It encapsulated a range of procedures, each with its own impenetrable acronym, all designed to delay or prevent people from applying for benefits—or, if that wasn't an option, to kick them off the rolls as quickly as possible.

There was EVR, the Eligibility Verification Review, wherein applicants were called to an office in Downtown Brooklyn and grilled to ensure the city considered them truly deserving of benefits. Failure to show up for the interview at the appointed time was considered an admission of guilt. There was FEDS, the Front End Detection System, in which one thousand five hundred city workers, including former police detectives, ran credit checks and knocked on applicants' doors unannounced, brandishing badges marked "FEDS" and demanding to know who lived there. At each step in the month-and-a-half application process, WAY handouts warned: "You will be terminated from your assignment and face severe sanctions if you: fail to report; have unexcused absences; fail to provide written documentation for absences; fail to cooperate with staff in assigned duties; fail to comply with regulations, policies or procedures at your work site."

While getting "diverted" sent a welfare recipient back to square one to start the application process all over again, being sanctioned was worse. Not only would applicants lose their welfare benefits for six months, but food stamps and Medicaid—federal entitlements available to anyone poor enough to qualify—would be cut off as well, on the presumption that anyone who had defrauded the system didn't deserve any financial help.

As applying for welfare became harder, getting sanctioned off the rolls got easier. Scheduled for two medical evaluations when only one was required? Miss the second, and that's a sanction. Skip a day of workfare to stay home with a sick child? Sanction. Miss an appointment because the notice was sent to an old address, or never sent at all? Sanction. At times, up to two-thirds of those engaged in workfare had been sanctioned off for one reason or another. Those who appealed to an administrative judge for "fair hearings," legal advocates for the poor noticed, won 80 percent of the time. If legal counsel accompanied them, the figure jumped to 98 percent.

In ruling against the city in one of the raft of lawsuits brought by antipoverty groups against Giuliani's welfare policies, Federal District Court Judge William Pauley III noted that some applicants for assistance had been rejected for failing to be in two places at the same time. This practice, the Urban Justice Center noted dryly in a report on the decision, was "especially problematic."

As it turned out, this was only the beginning.

* * *

With the arrival of Jason Turner as city welfare director in 1998, Giuliani's diversion policies were fully unleashed. Turner, a welfare reform evangelist who spoke to interviewers of spending his student days in a Connecticut high school doodling sketches of factories in which to put the poor to work, had masterminded Wisconsin's pioneering "W-2" workfare program, which slashed that state's rolls almost to zero. Upon arriving in New York from Wisconsin, he told WNYC public radio interviewer Brian Lehrer that "work will make you free," apparently unaware the phrase infamously appeared on the gates of Auschwitz. In a speech before the Manhattan Institute, Turner explained that the solution to swollen welfare rolls was "to create, if you will, a personal crisis in individuals' lives." The disciples he brought with him were, like him, formerly with conservative think tanks and well-versed in the mentality of "work first."

After his installation as commissioner of the city's Human Resources Administration—his predecessor, Lilliam Barrios-Paoli, had pushed for the addition of more vocational education and training opportunities for those on welfare, and was summarily dismissed by the mayor for lacking his "strong philosophical commitment" to the program's tenets—Turner promptly set out to convert the city's welfare offices into "Job Centers."

Applicants walking in the door of any of these renamed facilities were met with signs declaring "A JOB IS YOUR FUTURE. WELFARE IS TIME LIMITED. THE CLOCK IS TICKING," and paraded before a dizzying array of recommissioned city workers: the financial planning receptionist, the financial planner, the employment planner, each of whom was tasked to find a way, any way, to keep people from relying on welfare. (It was, in fact, part of their job description. Turner had issued an employee manual to Job Center workers, explaining that finding jobs for applicants was their "secondary goal"; the "primary goal" was diversion.)

In an interview, Krueger, who was elected to the New York state senate in 2002, recalled that Job Centers rewarded employees who racked up the biggest caseload reductions. "They had little parties with balloons each month—I'm not kidding," she said. "They got employee-of-the-month awards, and little signs over their desks." Oversized fundraising-style thermometers, she remembered, tracked each center's success at cutting caseloads.

Where red tape wouldn't do the trick, there was simple rudeness to fall back on. In the summer of 1998, as Turner's changes began to take hold, the nonprofit Urban Justice Center sent volunteers to stand outside Job Centers and interview applicants. One woman who had been forced by illness to leave her previous job said she'd been told by a caseworker, "I know you're in a hurry to go to your home or your husband or your pimp. . . . The worst thing you can do in your life is come here. You are dirt here; you are nothing." According to the UJC's report, she recalled thinking that "it was horrible . . . why is she doing this to us? If she wants me to get away from there, she got it."

From the point of view of the Giuliani administration, Turner's diversion efforts were a spectacular success. The Jamaica Job Center reported that in its first four weeks of operation, 84 percent of those who walked in the door walked right back out again without even filing an application. Overall rejection rates soared from 27 percent in the pre-Giuliani days to 57 percent in 1998; at the new Job Centers, three-quarters of those who managed to apply were being denied benefits. At the same time, just 5 percent of the first fifty-three hundred people who went through "job search" at the Job Centers had actually found jobs. Clearly, someone had been reading the manual.

As for what had become of all these people, the diverted and the sanctioned, it was an official mystery: The city made no effort to track their whereabouts. Turner's Human Resources Administration responded to all inquiries with a stony silence, and Giuliani insisted, with a straight face, that he didn't want to play "Big Brother." Richard Schwartz, the mayor's top welfare advisor during his first term, summed up City Hall's attitude: "If a quarter-million people removed from the rolls had no other place to go, you'd see homelessness increase. You'd see the crime rate go up. That hasn't happened."

At Columbia University's Social Indicators Survey Center, a group of demographers decided to attack the question of the missing welfare recipients from a new angle. Instead of trying to keep track of those leaving welfare, why not see how the poor as a whole were faring in the city in this anti-welfare era? The results of their little-known study were published in various papers between 2000 and 2004.[1] While the number of families leaving welfare each year had remained fairly constant under Giuliani, the number going on welfare was plummeting. At the same time, the number of families poor enough to qualify for welfare had dropped, but only slightly, from 21 percent to 19 percent between 1996 and 2001, and this at a time when the city's economy was booming.

New Yorkers weren't getting any less poor. They were just getting less welfare.

* * *

Even a decade later, it's impossible for researchers to know exactly how many people found jobs as a result of workfare. What is certain is that the number who found a job, temporary or otherwise, is low.

When pressed by reporters and members of the City Council, Turner's agency let slip figures that showed anywhere from 5 to 9 percent of those who were placed in workfare reported having found a real job, either through the city or on their own. (One HRA report, which claimed 18.5 percent of single parents and 15.1 percent of childless recipients had found regular jobs after leaving workfare, turned out to have counted as "successfully placed in employment" welfare cases that had been closed for very different reasons, as well as applications that were rejected or withdrawn.) The percentages looked dismal when considering that the poor find jobs, and often lose them again, all the time: An Urban Institute study in the pre–welfare reform 1980s found that 46 percent of those leaving the welfare system had found work.

Giuliani seemed unperturbed by all this. Asked by the *New York Times*'s Jason DeParle which was more important, getting people working or getting them off welfare, the mayor replied: "The most important number is decreasing the numbers of people dependent on the government to support them—because, after all, that really is government's role. . . . The first thing that I look at is considerably fewer numbers of people having to come to the government to say, 'Give me a check.'"

By then it was already clear that those people were turning elsewhere for help. Between 1995 and 1998, the number of people showing up each month at city food pantries and soup kitchens roughly doubled, from three hundred thousand to six hundred thousand, despite generally improving economic conditions. More than half of emergency food providers surveyed by Manhattan City Council member Gifford Miller's office reported they'd been forced to cut rations rather than turn people away. Nonetheless, people were being turned away from emergency food services in dramatically increasing numbers—fifty-nine thousand in January 1998 alone, a few months before the mayor's chat with DeParle.

Other indicators of distress were similarly on the rise. The Coalition for the Homeless reported that applications for emergency shelter had risen by 90 percent between 1995 and 1998. (The family shelter system would swell to record levels by the time Giuliani left office.) The city's subsidized day care program was flooded with new requests from parents forced to meet the new work require-ments. Even after the city added thirteen thousand new slots, the waiting list more than doubled, to twenty-four thousand kids.

In its survey of city residents, Columbia's SIS Center found that conditions were bleakest for those who were poor enough to receive welfare but were no longer getting aid. Among these families, aver-age income was down by $300 a year. The number of families with health insurance coverage had dropped 23 percent. Housing over-crowding was up "steeply," as was hunger. Missed or late utility pay-ments, utility shutoffs, being forced to double up with friends and relatives, all went up—though not for those still getting welfare. Within the City University of New York, meanwhile, enrollment fell by more than twenty thousand students, or one in ten students, with many reporting they had been forced to drop out when they could-n't juggle classes and coursework with their workfare assignment.

* * *

Giuliani's diversion tactics were proving so effective that applicants were diverted from programs that didn't cost the city a dime, such as food stamps, a federal program for which anyone, working or not, could apply. When advocates for the poor began noticing that food-stamp use had dropped 15 percent during Turner's first year, the new welfare chief waved it off, explaining that "the culture has changed."

In a sense, he was right, but it was the culture of the welfare bureaucrats, not of those they were serving. U.S. Department of Agriculture investigators found that applicants in the city were being routinely—and illegally—told they would need to do a job search before they could apply for food stamps. In the wake of this finding, Turner agreed to have the Job Centers begin providing food stamp applications, but a defiant-sounding Giuliani overruled him, saying, "Everything HRA is doing now is consistent with the welfare reform laws passed by Congress." That the federal government was telling him otherwise—telling the former federal prosecutor, in fact, that he might be breaking the law—had no evident impact on Giuliani.

For those who'd spent the better part of the Giuliani years bat-tling the mayor's poverty-related policies—the advocates and legal-aid attorneys whom Giuliani had memorably lumped together as "the apostles of dependency"—this sort of lawlessness was the last straw. Krueger, one of those who'd first tipped off the USDA to reports of plummeting food-stamp usage, remembered a late-night conference call with a USDA lawyer and a staff person for then–New York senator Daniel Patrick Moynihan. "We'd done everything," said Krueger. "We won. Except for the fact that New York City refused to change their policies."

Exasperated, she pressed the federal staffers: Now that it was clear that the Giuliani administration was breaking the law, what could they do to enforce it? "And they said, 'We don't know.' I said, 'Well, what's the precedent for this? For a local government refusing to follow federal law?'

"And the guy from the Senate said, 'Well, there was that prece-dent where we sent in the National Guard against George Wallace. But I'm not sure we're doing that again.'"

*

1. *Myers, M.K., and Naidich, W. (2001). After the Reforms: Welfare Recipients, Leavers, and Non-Recipients in New York City, 1996 and 1998. Social Indicators Survey Center Working Paper #01–02. New York: Columbia University School of Social Work.*

Meyers, M.K., W. J. Waldfogel, J., & Garfinkel, I. (2001) Child Care in the Wake of Welfare Reform: The Impact of Government Subsidies on the Economic Well-Being of Single Mother Families. Social Services Review, 75 (1), 29–59.

Myers, M.K. & Lee, J.W. (2002). Working but Poor: How Are Families Faring? Children and Youth Services Review, 25 (3), 177–201.

6

Largesse
Charles V. Bagli

ON A SULTRY August day, Rudolph Giuliani strode into the Blue Room of City Hall and announced that Bear Stearns & Company would build a new headquarters on Madison Avenue and his administration had agreed to give the global financial giant $75 million in tax breaks.

"Bear Stearns is very important to New York City's financial community," the mayor told reporters gathered for the press conference. "Whenever you see a development like this, it's a sign that the city's moving in the right direction."

Asked whether the city approved the tax breaks after Bear Stearns had threatened, like so many other major corporations, to abandon Manhattan, Giuliani dismissed the question as "silly."

"It doesn't matter," he snapped. "I don't really care."

Bear Stearns chief executive James E. Cayne, who could be as prickly as Giuliani, did care, however. He responded simultaneously to the reporter's question with an emphatic "No."

"I think it's idiotic to go down that road," Cayne told me a bit later when I asked him about it during an interview. "I'm not interested in going to Connecticut, New Jersey, or Tampa, Florida. We've been in New York for seventy-five years. This is our home."

It was late 1997. The city, indeed the country, was coming out of a long recession. The mayor and Cayne failed to mention that six years earlier, Bear Stearns had threatened to move its operations to

Whippany, New Jersey, and the threat had caused then-mayor David Dinkins to approve more than $37 million in tax abatements to keep the bank and at least 5,700 employees in New York City.

None of the reporters arrayed before Giuliani's podium in the Blue Room seemed to recall that. At least, none of us at the press conference asked why another offering of taxpayer-funded inducements was once again necessary. But my curiosity was piqued when, in a conversation with Bear Stearn's real estate lawyer Leonard Boxer a few moments before the press conference began, I learned that neither he nor the city's chief negotiator for "corporate retention deals," Ross Moskowitz, had been involved in working out the incentive package.

Not one of us in the press corps realized that the Giuliani administration's $75 million package was thrown together only the night before, during what some participants would describe as a cursory negotiation in an apartment behind the New York Mets owner's luxury box in Shea Stadium.

The origin of those secret talks, not to mention the setting for them, was rooted in the relationship between two men ostensibly on opposite sides of the bargaining table: Fred Wilpon, the owner of the Mets and a member of the board of directors for Bear Stearns, and Deputy Mayor for Economic Development Randy Levine, a gregarious lawyer whose close ties to Major League Baseball included a consulting contract and deferred income adding up to about $900,000, a one-year option to return to baseball, and a hot line on his City Hall desk to MLB's Park Avenue headquarters. Levine had been the chief labor negotiator for Major League Baseball and had answered to its executive committee, which included both Wilpon and George Steinbrenner. When some of the behind-the-scenes circumstances resulting in the tax break surfaced a year later in an article by Wayne Barrett in the *Village Voice*, it caused barely a ripple of public discussion. Wilpon and Levine said nothing untoward occurred in their talks concerning Bear Stearns.

The outcome was typical of the Giuliani years. The package of benefits for one of the largest and most profitable companies in the city marked the administration's thirty-third so-called corporate retention deal in less than four years, far outpacing Giuliani's two immediate predecessors and diverging little from some of the subsidies his fiscal team had given to CBS, Ernst & Young, Travelers, Conde Nast, Credit Suisse First Boston, and The New York Times Company. That the economy was emerging from a six-year slump by the time Bear Stearns approached City Hall for help mattered little and maybe not at all to a mayor determined to be viewed as pro-business.

By 1997 in New York, local companies were finished with shedding middle managers. They were expanding payrolls. Midtown Manhattan commercial property prices and rents were climbing. Occupancy rates, too, were going up. Even Lower Manhattan, which had been on the ropes, was going strong, and the stock market was gathering steam. The Roaring Late Nineties, irrational exuberance and all, were clearly afoot, in dramatic contrast to the earlier years of a decade known for downsizing and deficits.

Rents and real estate values were rising to such heights by the time the city and company officials got together in Wilpon's stadium apartment that a predictable countertrend was also under way, one that had affected New York in prior periods of rapid Wall Street–fueled expansion. Financial firms, publishers, and insurance companies were looking to Jersey City and Hoboken for cheaper and newer digs. Over the next three years, from 1997 to 2000, this trickle would become a torrent as Manhattan's notoriously high property costs leapt ever higher. Dozens of large corporations reacted by moving thousands of jobs west across the Hudson River.

Giuliani, who had been elected on a crime-fighting platform, was largely caught off guard. He contended that as long as chief executive officers believed that muggings, burglaries, and shootings were in remission, their businesses would invest in new buildings and hire more employees within the city. This was a reasonable argument, but the mayor's economic development thinking never went beyond that. And when companies approached City Hall with talk of leaving town in spite of the improving public safety and economic conditions in 1997, the Giuliani administration had but one response: Open the city's wallet, and ask very few questions.

As much as Giuliani was disinclined to debate with even the most constructive-sounding critics, his administration refused to readjust its economic-development notions to changing economic conditions. Many good-government groups, urban planners, and well-respected researchers said the city should have been developing lower-cost office districts outside of Manhattan to compete with New Jersey. It was sound and fairly basic advice, but it fell on deaf ears in City Hall.

Certainly Giuliani could have used his bully pulpit to prod Congress to impose sanctions against states and municipalities that used federal tax breaks to lure companies from one location to another. With the city entering a period of robust growth, the mayor had leverage to stem corporate tax breaks. Dinkins, who presided during a shrinking economy, a crack epidemic, and rampant violence, did not have the same freedom to operate. Far from playing hardball with the city's corporate citizens, Giuliani forgave more than $1 billion in taxes to the likes of Merrill Lynch and fifty other corporations that threatened to walk.

This was a telling contrast to Giuliani's image as the tough guy who fearlessly took on itinerant squeegee men, panhandlers, and sidewalk peddlers. Rudy was in reality often a pushover where the city's most powerful interests were concerned—that is, when they desired something from hard-pressed taxpayers.

Giuliani and his minions so popularized the concept of "corporate retention" that Clay Lifflander, the president of the city's tax-exempt Economic Development Corporation early in the Rudy years, boasted that the administration had worked out more corporate benefit deals faster and better than any other.

"There was no economic development policy," laments H. Claude Shostal, who was president of the Regional Plan Association, an urban-planning organization. "They threw all the incentives at the big guys and they didn't have anything left for the development of back office space, or the small and medium-size firms that generate a lot of job growth."

* * *

One of the problems the mayor blew past was that big companies rarely consider a public subsidy as a major factor in a decision on whether to relocate. The deals, though designed to retain a company's jobs and taxes, are often a waste of public resources that could better be spent on mass transit, roads, hospitals, and schools. They also serve to shift the tax burden toward small businesses, whose threats to leave town would not carry as much weight.

"The subsidies can turn out to be giveaways," explains James Hughes, dean of Rutgers University's School of Planning and Public Policy. "In many cases, you're providing a bonus for someone who would've taken the same course of action anyway."

Giuliani's succession of deputy mayors of economic development—John Dyson, Randy Levine, and Robert Harding— hardly invented the corporate retention deal. They were following a well-worn path established by Edward Koch and David Dinkins.

In the late 1970s, Mayor Koch sought to help the city out of a fiscal morass by offering developers a raft of incentives and zoning bonuses to stimulate the construction of office and residential spires in Midtown.

Later, during the economic boom of the mid-1980s, Koch's administration feared that Chase Manhattan Bank was on the verge of moving thousands of back office employees to the suburbs and that if one bank left, the rest would soon follow. He gave Chase $235 million, the single largest benefit package in municipal history, to move thousands of employees to Brooklyn.

Koch also granted a $100 million package of assistance to NBC, which had been making noises of its own about ditching Rockefeller Center for New Jersey. City officials justified this assistance by saying Chase and NBC wouldn't generate any more tax revenue for the city if they left town—better to give a little now than to be sorry later.

In 1989, the year Dinkins took office, the need for retention deals was driven in large measure by the national recession and real estate depression (local property values fell by 50 percent). Though perhaps difficult to imagine all these years later, there were three newly built skyscrapers standing vacant in then-seedy Times Square. And entire stretches of Broad Street in the Lower Manhattan financial district looked like a ghost town, prompting real estate developers to worry that many of the landmark buildings had outlived their usefulness.

Carl Weisbrod, then president of the city's Economic Development Corporation, says the Dinkins administration was haunted by a nightmarish vision of the financial district disintegrating. Well before e-mail and the Internet reshaped the workplace, pundits and futurists predicted that modern telecommunications would rapidly strip away the need for large businesses to congregate in major cities.

It was against that bleak backdrop that the Dinkins administration hammered out a $106 million deal to keep Prudential Securities downtown. (The company had threatened to relocate to Newark, New Jersey, home of its parent company, Prudential Insurance.) The administration also handed out $100 million in property-tax incentives to Morgan Stanley, an inducement for the firm to buy two of those empty skyscrapers in Times Square.

Before long, many other companies big enough to demand a "retention deal" got in line. One of the more memorable agreements materialized in 1993, when Dinkins granted $49.5 million in incentives to CBS. Quite candidly, Laurence Tisch, the network's chairman, drew a distinction between his company and any other one looking to bend the city over a barrel for subsidies.

"We never threatened to leave the city," he said. "I just wanted to be treated like everyone else."

Giuliani occasionally criticized these kind of deals as giveaways in his successful 1993 campaign for mayor. But he quickly embraced the tactics once he got into office. Corporate New York got the message. Almost routinely, whenever a large company's lease for office space was due to expire, it hired real estate brokers to ride out to Jersey City and solicit a proposal from a major developer such as Richard Lefrak (then building the vast Newport complex on the Hudson River waterfront). Then came handout time. "A lot of people come out and kick the tires and then go back to New York and negotiate a deal," Lefrak remarked at the time.

During the early days of the Giuliani administration, when the local economy was still in tatters, it may have been difficult to tell which company executives were bluffing and which were for real. But by the end of 1997, when Bear Stearns called on City Hall, it should have been easy.

Bear Stearns, in fact, scoured Midtown for years for a location to build new uptown headquarters. Cayne zeroed in on 383 Madison Avenue, where a vacant bank building covered an entire block. Its owner, the wealthy Albabtain family, initially rebuffed Cayne's offers to buy the prime parcel between Forty-sixth and Forty-seventh streets.

Wilpon was serving as a real estate adviser to Bear Sterns in addition to his role as a member of the investment bank's board of directors. He took members of the firm to look at Rock West, a site at the north end of Times Square. But it did not pan out either.

Finally, in the summer of 1997, Cayne and Wilpon offered a compromise to the Albabtains and began negotiations in earnest to lease the Madison Avenue site for ninety-nine years and build a million-square-foot home office on it. As the talks drew to a close that August, Wilpon, who had built hundreds of millions of dollars worth of projects in New York, later told me, he was not sure whom to approach at the Giuliani administration's Economic Development Corporation and had called a friend at City Hall for guidance.

"We reached out to Randy Levine when we needed to determine who to deal with within his organization," Wilpon said. "He put us in touch with Charlie Millard."

Charles Millard was then president of the Economic Development Corporation and reported to Levine at City Hall. Because of Levine's ties to Major League Baseball, the city's Conflict of Interest Board had barred Levine from participating in talks on building new stadiums for the Yankees or the Mets. All the same, the ethics panel did not bar him from negotiating with Mets owner Wilpon concerning Bear Stearns.

The day before Giuliani's August 27, 1997, press conference at City Hall with Bear Stearns executives, Levine dispatched Millard and Millard's chief deputy Eric Deutsch to Shea to negotiate a tax deal with the investment bank. According to participants in the meeting, they were met by Wilpon and the chief operating officer for Bear Stearns, William Montgoris.

"Randy said we've got to do this deal," recalled an Economic Development Corporation (EDC) official. "There were no records showing any meetings at EDC prior to the announcement because there weren't any. I was in my office until 10:00 that night running the numbers, while Eric and Millard were out at Shea Stadium."

If ever the city held the high cards in the high-stakes poker game of corporate retention, it was at this moment, with Bear Stearns. The company already had a prior agreement with the Dinkins administration committing it to remaining in New York, so it could not condition the deal on yet another tax break. The bank had just that morning signed a ninety-nine-year lease for the property. And finally, Bear Stearns was required under the lease with the Albabtains to build a new office tower.

But Millard and Deutsch were under orders to do a deal, and the unstated message from Wilpon was clear, according to one city official: Don't make me call Randy. In any event, Randy Levine was available by phone and Millard spoke to him at least once, the official said.

The talks were largely a calculation of corporate benefits. As *Larry King Live* played on television in the background, Wilpon spoke about his friendship with the talk show host and their shared roots in Brooklyn. He mentioned that he had persuaded King not to question his guest that night—Rudolph Giuliani—about the mayor's alleged affair with his City Hall press secretary, Cristyne Lategano, with rumors then making the rounds despite both parties' assertions that they were never romantic partners.

As the negotiations went well into the night, the Mets lost to the San Francisco Giants, six to two. The city's taxpayers lost, too. Bear Stearns was granted $45 million in sales tax exemptions in return for maintaining 5,700 employees in New York City. The bank was allowed to collect another $30 million in benefits if its payroll soared to a projected 13,300, a wishful if not outlandish figure, given the cycles of the economy, and the slowdowns that inevitably follow each boom.

But the Giuliani administration's assistance to Bear Stearns did not end there. The city's Planning Department helped shepherd through a winding approval process the bank's plans for a forty-five-story headquarters, making critical decisions along the way that allowed the bank to build a larger skyscraper on the site than the zoning would ordinarily allow. In doing so, it did not require Bear Stearns to build in some of the costly public amenities routinely associated with tall buildings, noted Kevin Finnegan, who was the zoning chairman with the neighborhood's community board.

In all, the Giuliani administration's corporate retention deals, many of them struck during what was arguably the biggest real estate boom in city history, cost the city taxpayers an average of $125 million per year, far exceeding the rate of spending of any other mayor in this regard. The total would have exceeded $2 billion, or $250 million a year, if Giuliani's push to build a new trading complex for the New York Stock Exchange had not fallen apart. By comparison, Dinkins, in an unremittingly bad economy, granted $228 million in four years, an average of $57 million a year.

As the Giuliani years were in many ways grab-bag years for corporate interests, critics can be forgiven for describing the administration's generosity as excessive, lacking in nuance or finesse, and virtually indiscriminate.

For example, though the city had granted CBS nearly $50 million in corporate retention tax breaks in the late 1980s, the Giuliani team tossed in $10 million extra—no problem—after the company said it was considering relocating to Lefrak's Newport complex in Jersey City. The network thus received a second helping of subsidies even though it had failed to live up to the terms of its first agreement, when CBS had pledged to spend $300 million to upgrade its studios on West Fifty-seventh Street with digital equipment; six years later, the work had barely begun.

When, a year after the $10 million stipend, the Giuliani administration failed to convince Chase Manhattan Bank to keep thousands of jobs based in Lower Manhattan, some city officials argued that the Chase deal illustrated the risk of ignoring corporate threats to relocate, especially with prime office space in Manhattan renting for a premium $50–60 per square foot and Jersey City beckoning with far more affordable leases and construction costs as well as its own set of lucrative tax breaks. The argument had resonance, but at the same time, many urban planners and even some real estate developers had a very different take on Chase's decision to leave New York. The bank's departure, they said, showed the city's folly in having failed to foster a more comprehensive economic development approach. Companies were looking for sites to build custom office buildings and to lower business costs. The sites in New Jersey were ready to go. Lefrak, in fact, promised Chase that he'd build the bank a new space in eighteen months—eighteen months faster than anyone could have imagined happening in New York City. The city had allowed itself to lag in a highly competitive situation, and the lag only worsened in the Giuliani years. While New Jersey officials never tired of extolling the economic benefits of its waterfront to corporate executives in Manhattan, there was no competing marketing campaign by the Giuliani administration flagging the convenient train rides from Midtown to Long Island City, Queens, or Downtown Brooklyn. There were no ready-made development sites or the proper zoning at these locations to enable a builder to put up a back-office building in eighteen months.

* * *

The single largest deal of the Giuliani era, the mother of them all, took place more than a year after the Bear Stearns deal.

It was December 1998, and Giuliani was trumpeting what he described as a "Christmas gift" to the city: the New York Stock Exchange had agreed to build a state-of-the-art trading complex and fifty-story office tower on an entire block across the street from the Exchange's historic home on Wall Street. The mayor said the blockbuster deal would ensure that the Stock Exchange would remain downtown, within the third-largest business district in the country, and New York City would remain the financial capital of the world.

"This is a significant investment on the part of the city and the state," he said, "and is easily justified by the returns it will create for the city because it will keep the financial sector's center of gravity in Lower Manhattan and will solidify our role as the financial capital of the world."

Reporters who asked Giuliani that same day to say why the city was giving a billion dollars worth of assistance to one of the richest financial institutions in the world were, of course, chastised for their "knee-jerk" inquiries. Giuliani and Levine asserted (inaccurately, it turned out, as more details of the deal emerged) that the cost was not anywhere close to $1 billion; it was in fact much more.

By the end of the mayor's time in office, the holiday present offered by Giuliani to New Yorkers had become a lump of coal under spiraling costs, Stock Exchange hubris, and the widespread fear of skyscrapers in the wake of 9/11. By 2002, the city, which had taken on most of the initial risks and costs of the project, had spent $109 million trying to turn the deal into a reality.

It's worthwhile, I think, to look closely at the rise and fall of what came to be viewed widely as something of a fiasco.

The New York Stock Exchange had complained for at least a decade that its Wall Street home was cramped and antiquated. It had sought several alternatives, including building a new trading complex nearby and renovating space in other buildings. NYSE executives had also threatened to move to New Jersey, where officials were all but promising to build a new headquarters for free in Jersey City.

The Giuliani administration, led by Levine, Dyson, and Planning Department chairman Joseph Rose, crafted an agreement to build the Stock Exchange a new trading complex on the block bound by Wall, Broad, and William Streets and Exchange Place. The complex would incorporate J. Pierpont Morgan's landmark Morgan Guaranty Trust Company building but required demolishing several buildings occupied by J.P. Morgan as well as an apartment building that had recently been used for offices.

The city agreed to provide $160 million in tax breaks and $480 million in cash for the tower, plus a projected $450 million for the acquisition of the block bounded by Wall, Broad, and Williams Streets and Exchange Place. The Stock Exchange, in turn, was committed to spending $350 million or so to outfit the trading floors.

The beauty of it, said Levine, was that the city would sell the rights to build the tower over the trading complex in return for a rent that would cover the cost of buying the land. That, at any rate, was the plan. But the project came under attack by Wall Street analysts, urban planners, and civic groups. Some critics questioned the Exchange's heavy investment in traditional trading floors for stock trading at a time when electronic trading was coming to the fore. Although the Internet accounted for a small percentage of all trading in the United States, investors were increasingly using their own computers to buy stocks, while major exchanges in London and Frankfurt had already made the leap to electronic trading. In a comment that, typically, went unheeded by Giuliani, Mitchell Moss, the director New York University's Urban Research Center, described the deal at the time as "a high-risk investment for both the city and the state."

The region's good-government groups were sufficiently experienced with the false promise of what they often called "corporate welfare" that some questioned the plausibility of the Stock Exchange's threat to abandon New York for New Jersey. They pointed out that the city already had provided hundreds of millions of dollars in tax breaks to Morgan Stanley, Bear Stearns, and other influential members of the Stock Exchange to ensure the financial industry did not move lock, stock, and barrel out to the suburbs. Why would the investment banks now turn around and vote to move the Stock Exchange to New Jersey? Such a decision would not only inconvenience them, but quite possibly it would also undermine their New York real estate investments.

Negotiations between the city and the Stock Exchange dragged into 2000, and the anticipated costs of the project soared. Developers who had been solicited by the city refused to meet the city's conditions—to build the fifty-story office tower whether or not they were they were able to sign up an anchor tenant for the office space. The city, meanwhile, signed an agreement to buy the buildings from JP Morgan and to purchase the apartment building on the site and relocate the tenants.

Behind the scenes, Governor George Pataki's administration, no fan of Giuliani's grandstanding, began grousing about what it thought was the mayor's prodigious generosity toward the Stock Exchange. Charles Gargano, chairman of the state's Empire State Development Corporation, essentially wiped his hands of the land deal and refused to contribute more cash than the state's original offer of $225 million. That left the city with an ever larger pile of project expenses to cover.

The whole sorry chapter ended in the gloom and trauma after September 11, 2001, when every office building downtown looked like a potential target. Richard Grasso, then chairman of the Stock

Exchange, would say the fifty-story office building over the trading complex "was not a salable transaction"—knocking out whatever financial underpinning the project still had left.

Nonetheless, in a bid for an outsize capstone to memorialize his mayoralty, the Giuliani administration spent the last days of 2001 desperately trying to close the deal with Grasso in time for another one of those triumphal press conferences. Giuliani hoped to stage the announcement not in the Blue Room of City Hall, but at the Stock Exchange itself. And then, right after the announcement, he would ring the opening bell, signaling the last day of trading of the year, and, in this case, the last day of his tenure as "America's mayor."

It was just the kind of event that would have pleased the self-congratulatory, legacy-conscious Rudolph W. Giuliani, but even with the city's enormous public reserves at his disposal, and his amply demonstrated propensity to be generous toward corporate New York, it never happened.

7

Instruction
LynNell Hancock

I WITNESSED PLENTY of over-the-top scenes from my front-row press seat in the musty public hearing hall at 110 Livingston Street's Board of Education headquarters. At one tempestuous meeting in the early nineties, a Queens parent clicked his heels and saluted Schools Chancellor Joseph Fernandez, Hitler-style. The topic, I recall, was Fernandez's suggestion that first grade teachers include books like *Heather Has Two Mommies* in their multicultural lessons on families. On another volatile occasion, an evangelical preacher railed from the speaker's podium about the sins of providing condoms to high school students for HIV prevention. Carrying a worn Bible under his arm like an ecclesiastical Smith & Wesson, the minister bellowed to a heckler: "I hope you die of AIDS."

I would often distract myself at such moments by imagining the students in my own children's public school in the Bronx rolling their eyes at these self-absorbed adults and wondering why they weren't obsessed with things that really mattered, like real libraries, smaller classes, or safe places for recess.

But I think the oddest event at that time could neither be seen nor heard. In the midst of these mind-numbing culture wars over sex, death, and gender politics, it soon became clear that a shadowy influence was working the edges of the conservative social agenda. A Republican mayoral candidate, Rudolph Giuliani, had managed to quietly win over a once left-wing Latina community activist on the seven-member school board, convincing her to work on his campaign. From that moment on, the board's Bronx representative joined what became known as "The Gang of Four," a conservative majority. This voting bloc of Giuliani supporters would eventually drum the East Harlem–born schools chancellor out of town. Fernandez would represent Giuliani's first chancellor casualty—his most indirect, but not his last.

The strategic chutzpah was vintage Rudy. The mayoral candidate associated himself with the moralizing minority in order to help build his voting base among core constituents in conservative neighborhoods of Queens, Brooklyn, and Staten Island. He was behaving as if the New York mayor was expected to control school decisions, albeit from under the table. The end run against Fernandez was mayoral politics at its most shameless and a harbinger of fierce and furtive battles to come.

As soon as he took office in 1994, Giuliani suited up for full-scale rhetorical combat against the nation's largest public school system. Early on, he actually traveled to Albany to lobby for *less* school aid than the notoriously stingy State Legislature typically allocated. The mayor reasoned that he could not legitimately ask for billions of dollars during a fiscal crisis for a system he was accusing of chronic mismanagement. His unprecedented request would have effectively starved an already malnourished school system. More than five years later, Giuliani declared the schools to be so hopeless that "the whole system should be blown up." Never renowned for his tact, this outburst came only days after the Columbine High School massacre in Colorado, a time when the image of explosions in schools was particularly touchy.

Nothing much had changed since the candidate's stealth attack on Fernandez. If he couldn't have full control of the schools himself, then he would wear them down with backseat bullying. Keeping the Board of Education off balance with random assaults served his goal of controlling the schools in spite of state laws that were meant to keep City Hall politics at a safe distance from the one million mostly minority public schoolchildren.

Almost from his first days in office, in fact, Giuliani began battering the education system, highlighting its weaknesses and undermining public confidence in its ability to function, even on the simplest level. His outrage may have been welcomed if parents believed it came from a place of caring. But his attacks were rarely accompanied by substantive solutions. Looking back over those eight years of contentiousness, the mayor's education legacy added up to one of deliberate destruction. His most lasting contribution to the school system, even according to his supporters, was dismantling the old way of doing business to make way for the new.

"He discredited the institution in order to make a case for change," said Joseph Viteritti, Hunter College professor of education and a former Giuliani advisor. "The political consensus for mayoral control changed under his leadership."

That battle was won in the end, just not during his tenure. The pieces for reform fell into place when Giuliani's successor won Albany's blessing to eliminate the long-suffering Board of Education. But the final product has remained a work under scrutiny. Few had thought through the details or consequences of a City Hall takeover. Was it enough to have mayoral control at the top without community input from the school level? Were the schools simply exchanging one set of self-serving politics for another? And what precisely was there left to govern after eight years under Giuliani?

Some clues can be found by looking into Giuliani's school records. Should he be remembered as a leader who altered the governing structure of public education in the city? Or as an ambitious politician with half a plan and a two-by-four?

* * *

Few questioned the need for a radical overhaul of the school system by the time Giuliani was inaugurated. New York City schools had languished for years under an inept and unwieldy bureaucracy. Many of its thirty-two decentralized school boards had bartered away their agenda to the special interests of the teachers union, local political clubhouses, and, in a few scattered neighborhoods, ultraconservative evangelists. A few superintendents, principals, and school board members felt free to plunder school coffers, using the education system as their personal hiring hall. The corrosive impact on learning was incalculable. Ever since the state began keeping track of its worst schools, New York City's overwhelmingly dominated the list.

In many ways, Giuliani carried the right resume for the job of school reformer. He swept into office wielding the same good-government hammer his mentor Mayor Fiorello La Guardia used to rid city politics of the rule of local political bosses. A former federal prosecutor who took down the corrupt Bronx Democratic machine, Giuliani promised to puncture the complacent education bureaucracy's bloat, to purge school corruption, to take mayoral responsibility for the schooling of the city's children.

At first, his challenge was a welcome jolt. Even former Mayor David Dinkins's supporters were grateful that a dragon slayer was finally willing to take on the torpid bureaucracy of 110 Livingston Street.

In time, Giuliani managed to install some useful ideas, such as better financial accounting on the school level, better access to textbooks, and private funding for sports fields. More prominent, though, were his hot-button prescriptions popular with the GOP, including tuition vouchers for private and parochial schools, police in schools, and grade retention. But Giuliani's attention span for the complexities of school reform was fleeting. He was perpetually distracted by his lack of operational control over the school system.

Every New York mayor since John Lindsay has vied for such control. It makes managerial sense since a mayor cannot be held accountable for the city's schools if he has no power over them. Lindsay was the first mayor to be stripped of that authority under the 1969 state education law creating thirty-two community school boards. Lindsay's penchant for community control worried Albany legislators and teachers union officials. Teachers' rights could be compromised if Lindsay moved to place parents in charge of things like school-based hiring decisions.

So, the law dispersed power in a rather helter-skelter fashion between the five borough presidents who chose one Board of Education member apiece and the mayor who chose two. Thirty-two elected community school boards were supposed to represent local interests but were given very little authority. This crazy quilt of mixed messages was called decentralization, even though power was never truly dispersed to the local districts.

Frustrated at being left impotent in the margins, many mayors since that time have treated the school system like an unpleasant drain on city funds. Some have cut its budget disproportionately compared to other city agencies. But no one did so more egregiously than Giuliani.

Rudy's first move in 1994 was to ask Fernandez's successor, Chancellor Ramon Cortines, for a list of 2,500 administrators to fire from central headquarters. He needed the cuts in order to withhold $754 million in operating funds in his deficit-plagued first year, and $548 million the second. Some school advocates applauded the accountability measures. "At first, I was happy to see him turning his attention where it should be, on the central administration," said John Fager, then co-chair of Parents Coalition of Education, an advocacy group. "He was going right after the source of the problem."

It soon became apparent that the public schools were required to squeeze out more than their fair share of dollars. Giuliani asked the schools to absorb $1.3 billion in cuts over two years while the fire and police department budgets were spared the ax. It would be next to impossible to weather such deep losses without affecting the classroom. "There is just so much that can be absorbed administratively," said Noreen Connell, executive director of the Education Priorities Panel, a respected research group. "In short order, the money starts coming out of playgrounds, bookshelves, and replacement light bulbs."

"It's one thing to attack 110 Livingston Street," said Fager. "It's another to have a real vision for changes to come."

Elementary school principals reported eliminating arts, music, and afterschool activities such as foreign language clubs and debate teams. Once gone, such classes are difficult to restore. Kindergarten class sizes soared to twenty-five children with only one teacher—a ratio considered harmful to the youngest children. Studies show the chaos of sharing one teacher among twenty-five little ones can cause not only social and academic delays but also dangerous situations. This is why the city's Health Department had devised strict codes more than forty years earlier, requiring one teacher for fifteen kindergartners and a paraprofessional for no more than ten additional children. The Board of Education historically has tried to wriggle around the requirements, but the Giuliani administration went so far as to eliminate them. The mayor demanded a permanent change in the Health Code to exempt the city's schools, a move that went practically unnoticed.

If the youngest children were hit hard under Giuliani, high school students took an even larger share of the blows. Some high school principals resorted to shortening more and more students' instructional days to absorb Giuliani's first-term 20 percent budget cuts. In his second year in office, one in four high school students were being sent home every day without the required five and a half hours of instruction. This came at the same time the state raised the standards for high school graduation to include rigorous Regents exams in all major subjects. Kids entering ninth grade already behind would have fewer chances to catch up, thus jeopardizing their odds for a diploma.

The state's education commissioner became so alarmed he ordered an investigation of the city's high school schedules. Commissioner Richard Mills found that some students were allowed a shortened day because they were over seventeen, or were only a few credits shy of graduation. Another sixty severely over-crowded schools were exempted because there was literally not enough time in the day to run split sessions and offer all the required courses. But a remaining seventy-five thousand students were being cheated out of class time solely to save money. "We cannot balance the budget on the backs of our high school students," Mills's associate commissioner told the *New York Times* in January 1996. On one hand, educators were telling students that a high school diploma was essential in life, she said. On the other, they were not providing all the coursework the students needed to graduate.

Giuliani's aides insisted that the school budget was never cut; rather, the operating expenses continued to inch upwards during his mayoralty. True, in part. The overall budget rose from $7.5 billion to $10 billion over Giuliani's two terms. But this modest increase did not reach the children until the very end of his tenure. The city's comptroller reports show that the school system annually spent $8,682 per student in 1993, David Dinkins's last year in office.

Spending did not reach that level again until six years into Giuliani's administration, when it surpassed it at $9,147 per pupil, according to New York University economics professor Emanuel Tobier. During roughly the same period, enrollment grew by eighty thousand students, many of them children of new immigrants.

In fact, as *Newsday* reported in April 1997, Giuliani "restricted the flow of money to the schools more severely than any mayor since the city's fiscal crisis of the mid-1970s."

Chancellor Cortines tried his best to defend the schools from draconian measures. He was particularly offended by City Hall's attempts to micromanage his personnel decisions. The former San Francisco school superintendent was operating from a distinct disadvantage when it came to the macho mayor. Giuliani simply didn't like him. Cortines was stiff and proper, not the kind of fellow the mayor could imagine enjoying a game with in Yankee Stadium or sharing a corpulent cigar and a good laugh.

When the chancellor showed up alone at City Hall with a list of only seven hundred names to fire and promises of five hundred more through attrition, the mayor lost all patience. Giuliani was serious about putting twice that many administrators on the chopping block. Cortines countered that the demand would destabilize an already vulnerable system. The mayor called his chancellor "the little victim," admonishing him not to "be so precious" when it came to taking criticism. The ugly sparring did not abate until Cortines finally gave up and quit in October 1995.

* * *

Giuliani relished his conquering role. He was comfortable battling in the volatile arenas of power, snapping off controversial decisions with ease. These tactics were fine for vanquishing murderers and car thieves. But they seemed out of place in the city's classrooms. Predictably, education became the mayor's most pronounced political liability. Early polls showed the public was growing weary of his random ideas and even more random pot shots. He made the obligatory school rounds as a candidate for re-election in 1997, angling his bulky frame into a child-size chair, and reading in singsongese before the cameras to clusters of elementary students at his feet.

It was a stroke of ironic fortune that Rudy Crew was hired by Giuliani's opponents on the Board of Education to be Cortines's replacement. The two men ended up sharing more than a first name. An affable African American with a lifelong love of the Yankees and a healthy thirst for a good sociable scotch, Crew became the mayor's buddy. His presence meant Giuliani finally had the kind of education leader who could help him make a mark. It didn't hurt that unprecedented national prosperity continued unabated in the mayor's second term. And school enrollment leveled off by the late nineties to manageable numbers. This was the perfect time to articulate an educational philosophy, to make a meaningful investment in the schools. He could become known for big-picture reforms: reducing overcrowding, attracting and nurturing quality teachers, building more schools, and keeping class sizes small.

Instead, Giuliani's education ideas—like most of his administration's agenda in his second term—remained slight, flavored by political rather than public interests. His pet project—putting the police department in charge of school security—slid through the channels of review and approval without much protest. Past chancellors had balked at the prospect of giving police authority to patrol school hallways. It was a signal that the school had lost its leadership. Crew managed to stop detectives from collecting every school's class yearbooks to aid in police investigations—a move favored by Giuliani that would have violated students' privacy. But the chancellor welcomed the NYPD takeover of the notoriously mismanaged security force. The door was now open for the possibility that students could be arrested for minor disputes ordinarily relegated to the principal's office.

Without consulting his friend, the mayor added $12 million to his 1999 budget for a voucher program that offered public money to children for parochial and private school tuition. The maneuver was inexplicable. "Giuliani is a lawyer," said Connell, the schools' watchdog. "He certainly knew there was no legal way that a taxpayer voucher program could fly in the state of New York." Even more puzzling, pushing vouchers was sure to alienate the chancellor, a vocal opponent of any programs that took children and money out of the public schools. The only explanation for this surreptitious announcement was strategy. Giuliani was seriously contemplating a run for U.S. Senate. He needed to burnish his image as a rightward Republican on the national stage, and he was never more focused than when the goal was personal power.

Almost on cue, Giuliani and the chancellor began a public feud so loud and destructive that it drowned out all fights that had came before it. Giuliani's aides thought by then that Crew was a zero as an educator. Crew decided that his mayor had only higher office on his mind. By the end of April 1999, Giuliani lost all civility and suggested that the schools be bombed (with figurative weapons). Crew responded in a public letter:

> When the Mayor declares that the whole school system should be blown up, he tells 1.1 million children and thousands of parents, teachers and administrators that they are wasting their time in schools that he has suddenly dismissed as no good and beyond redemption.
>
> We will not succeed in this genuinely American mission by sending a handful of children to parochial and other private schools with vouchers. We will not succeed by placing the public school system under the control of any one Mayor and any one political party. We will not succeed by engaging in reckless statements that discourage vibrant new teachers from signing up to work here.

Crew would never survive such an attack. Two days before Christmas 1999, the mayor put together four votes on the board to dump the former Tacoma, Washington, superintendent of schools. The third chancellor in six years disappeared, leaving the schools in their most unstable condition of Giuliani's tenure. But Crew did not leave before he had set in motion Giuliani's most ambitious education plan.

Social promotion—the practice of moving children through the grades without teaching them much of anything—is indefensible by anyone's measure. The debatable question is how to stop it. The most popular method is to hold the lowest achieving students back a grade. More long-lasting solutions are rarely considered, such as ensuring small class sizes and guaranteeing qualified teachers in the earliest grades. "The problem is all the failure is placed on the children's heads," said Fager, the parent advocate, "and not on the schools where it belongs." Punishment almost always packs a more potent political punch than prevention.

Chicago had tried grade retention. So had Philadelphia, Milwaukee, Baltimore, Washington DC, and twenty-one other school districts nationwide. New York City once had a massive "Gates" program under Chancellor Frank Macchiarola in the early 1980s that kept children back in the fourth and eighth grades. It cost as much as $60 million per year and was eventually scrapped as an ineffective waste of money.

None of these programs worked. And all were enormously expensive. They all depended on the fragile and often unreliable measure of disparate standardized tests. Research showed that holding kids back increases dropout rates and special education enrollment and does little to boost children's academic achievement. Strangely enough, even those children who slipped through the cracks and were promoted by mistake tested higher than those who repeated the grade.

Giuliani was aware of these findings. But some of his advisors convinced him the failures were due to neglectful leadership. The idea held a natural appeal for a mayor who had no education feathers in his national campaign platform. Holding children accountable gelled with his strong work ethic and his sense of personal responsibility. It was a way to prove that he could at last focus some of the city's economic windfall on curriculum measures, not just marginal ideas.

The mayor took so-called social promotion to its grandest extreme, implementing it in six consecutive grades, third through eighth, at a cost the Education Priorities Panel estimated to be $564 million per year. By the time Giuliani's fourth chancellor, Harold Levy, took office, central headquarters was completely absorbed in trying to make this unsound program work. It was, in the end, a squandered opportunity to invest in long-lasting change. "You can't blow that kind of money in Scarsdale," said Connell. "People would complain when it came up empty."

The clearest indication that Giuliani's exorbitant policy was an academic bust came five years later, at a post-Giuliani mayoral press conference. The newest chancellor, Joel Klein, lamented that 37 percent of the city's ninth graders were failing. "We can't continue the way we're going," Klein told reporters, "which is pushing children through the elementary schools." Mayor Michael Bloomberg, the first mayor in more than thirty years to hold direct authority over the schools, then announced his new idea. He would launch a program to keep failing children back in the third grade. The price tag for the extra year and the extra resources would weigh in at about $116 million annually. No one noted that these ninth graders had already been subjected to Giuliani's far more sweeping grade retention plan for six straight years. Obviously, for these kids, it did not work. The press was seized by collective amnesia; the politicians, by a need to make a high-decibel splash.

Bloomberg, who took office in 2001, staked his mayoralty on the successes or failures of public education—a bold banner to wave for any politician. As he looked ahead to his re-election bid, he needed a punchy program to convince voters he was serious. Until this point, Bloomberg had used his unprecedented power to overhaul the governing scaffolding of the schools, something Giuliani wanted desperately to do himself. He dismantled 110 Livingston Street and moved central headquarters next to City Hall. He aggressively pushed for small class sizes, more small schools, and across-the-grades arts education. He rearranged the age-old local districts into ten regions under his authority. The Board of Education was replaced by a less visible thirteen-member Panel on Education Policy, eight of them hand-picked by the mayor, five by parents.

Gone were the traditional squabbles between the mayor and chancellor over the schools' fair share of the city coffers. But gone too was a meaningful sense of community access to decisions affecting their schools. That loss became painfully evident in March 2004. Three of Bloomberg's appointees on the Panel on Education Policy made it clear that they would vote with the five parents against the mayor's retention plan because it held no educational value. It was the first time the inscrutable group refused to use its rubber stamp. Bloomberg responded promptly by firing the three defectors, replacing them with guaranteed yes voters. It was a Lewis Carroll "off-with-their-heads" kind of moment, more reminiscent of Giuliani's style and substance than that of his more subdued successor.

In retrospect, Bloomberg's sad display of democracy bashing was almost inevitable. Giuliani had created the role of the imperious mayor as school chief, someone who could be expected to care more about personal politics than education when an election was approaching. He had hammered together the scaffolding for mayoral control in his image, with little thought as to how it would work or whom it would affect. Control was his only goal, not creating lifelong learners among the city's schoolchildren. Bloomberg's ensuing display of raw power exposed the flaws of Giuliani's legacy, making me almost long for the days of brimstone preachers and zealous parents snapping off Nazi salutes. At least then the pretense that schools belonged to the public and not the politicians was still alive.

8

Economy
James Parrott and
David Dyssegaard Kallick

THE MAYORALTY OF Rudolph Giuliani coincided with one of the most powerful periods of economic growth in the country's recent history. The stock market was booming, the gross domestic product was soaring, and jobs were being created at a record pace.

In New York City, national headquarters for the finance industry and a center of the dot-com boom, wealth was accumulating even faster than in the rest of the country. The city government, in turn, realized the fullest fruits of the economic expansion in the form of record budget surpluses during Giuliani's second term.

Yet when it was time for the fortunate mayor to exit City Hall, the city's poverty rate actually was higher than a decade before. The middle class had lost ground, with the median wage having dipped by 3.7 percent during the 1990s in New York City, even as it grew by 5.7 percent in the nation. The local economy was more dependent than ever on a single, historically volatile industry—Wall Street. The city's long-term capital debt, rather than being pared during these flush times, was increased, leaving a huge debt service burden that consumed seventeen cents of every dollar in Giuliani's last annual budget. The next mayor, Michael Bloomberg, had to borrow $1.5 billion and raise property taxes by 18.49 percent to cover shortfalls in his first municipal budget that were caused not only by 9/11 but also by Giuliani's shortsighted budget policies.

Politicians, no matter what their status, like to take credit for good times. (The bad times? Well, they're invariably someone else's fault.) But even the crusading Giuliani didn't control enough of the economic levers to deserve top billing in the boom. In the middle and late 1990s, the high-flying stock market and dot-com phenomenon—both well beyond City Hall's influence—were key to buoying up a local economy still shaking off the effects of a brutal recession. The world financial markets fed a Wild West mentality on Wall Street, and the economy was further fired up by low interest rates and waves of immigrants who brought the city a mix of entrepreneurial spirit, professional skills, and an expanded workforce.

The right question in assessing Giuliani's economic legacy is not whether he created the boom economy. He didn't. Rather, the question is, *How did Giuliani play the excellent economic hand he was dealt?* By that measure, the major story of the Giuliani years constitutes, all in all, a missed opportunity that may not come around again for a very long time.

The symptoms of this lapse were serious. While some other cities experienced widely shared benefits from the economic gains of the 1990s, New York saw increased income polarization. The wealth that coursed through New York in the Giuliani years found its way into the hands of the fortunate minority at the top of the income ladder. The average New Yorker experienced rising costs of living, especially for housing, and lower (inflation adjusted) income levels. The median family income—a good gauge of how the middle class was doing—declined by 6 percent, compared to a 9.5 percent rise in median family income nationally.

Likewise, the portion of the city population living below the federally defined poverty line rose in the 1990s from 19.3 to 21.2 percent. Nationally, the poverty rate fell, from 13.1 to 12.4 percent.

The good news was that by the end of the 1990s, the unemployment rate was low for white New Yorkers, at 3.6 percent in 2000, though not for blacks and Hispanics, at 7.5 percent and 8 percent, respectively. But the bad news was that holding a job—or even two jobs—was often insufficient to keep a family securely above the poverty line. As for middle-class New Yorkers in particular—considered a central part of the mayor's constituency—the Giuliani years were no picnic. By 1999 the median income in New York City ranked twenty-second out of the forty biggest cities in the United States, lagging behind not only economic hotspots such as San Jose and San Francisco, but also Columbus, Indianapolis, Charlotte, and Washington DC.

Why did low-income as well as middle-income New Yorkers fare so much worse than their counterparts in the rest of the country?

A good place to begin is with the Giuliani administration's stringent rules for those seeking public assistance, whether food stamps or welfare checks. His high-profile Work Experience Program, or WEP, pushed thousands of welfare recipients into unpaid work assignments without training or education to help them get decent-paying jobs of their own. Indeed, thousands were forced to drop out of college to show up for workfare assignments. WEP was initiated in the spring of 1995, at a time when even downsized middle managers were having trouble finding work, and more than a year before Congress passed work requirements for welfare recipients nationally.

In the years following Giuliani's rollout of what became the largest workfare contingent in the country—with as many as thirty-three thousand orange-vested welfare recipients working for their public assistance benefits at any one time—a study by the Urban Institute detected some of the first broad, deleterious effects on the fortunes of working New Yorkers. The report found that the hourly wages of single mothers with no college degree fell from $8 an hour in 1995–96 to $7.08 in 1998–99, a decline of 11.5 percent in just three years. In effect, the report stated, they were competing with people turned down for relief checks under the city's tough new rules for obtaining assistance. What resulted was a buyer's market for employers looking for inexpensive help. The surfeit of applicants, fed by a sizable reduction in the welfare rolls, helped employers cut wages.

To make matters worse, the Giuliani administration reversed the role that city government traditionally played in setting the salary standard for low-level employees. To begin with, Giuliani froze wages for all city workers in the mid-1990s in negotiations with unions representing city government employees. The workfare program also had a corrosive effect on low-end salaries around the city, with public assistance recipients "earning" in their welfare checks less than the minimum wage of $5.15 per hour for their assigned duties. What is more, the welfare labor force displaced the ranks of civil servants who had previously raked, mopped, swept, and filed for the government. "The city's largest sweatshop" was how Community Voices Heard, a grassroots group that advocated on behalf of workfare assignees, aptly described the workfare juggernaut.

Over time, Giuliani's policies governing $5 billion worth of city-contracted social services contributed, as well, to pulling wages downward. The administration's failure to provide raises for an estimated one hundred thousand private-sector social service employees who worked under contracts originating with the city meant that in time, these workers lost ground vis-à-vis the rising cost of living. Giuliani also laid off or otherwise displaced thousands of the city's social and health services workers, resulting in a 15 percent decline in black female employment and a 10 percent drop in black male employment in mayoral agencies as a whole.

* * *

Economists' central concern about the New York economy has been its chronic over-reliance on Wall Street. Five percent of the New York City workforce had jobs in the finance sector in the 1990s, yet that sector accounted for 48 percent of the city's economic growth between 1992 and 2000, compared to 16 percent during the boom years of the 1980s. Dependence on Wall Street brings in its wake greater inequality between rich and poor, over-inflated real estate prices (due to the high salaries commanded by people working in the finance industry), and dizzying volatility as the economy swings with stock prices.

While revenues were flowing in from Wall Street, Giuliani could have been investing them in education and job training in growing fields such as health care in order to build a labor pool that would give the city a competitive edge in emerging sectors. He also could have accomplished what cities such as Milwaukee have done, offering clusters of companies government support and discounted office space and equipment to incubate and cultivate industries that can get a foothold in the city. To chart the path toward economic diversification, Giuliani also would have done well to follow through on the beginnings of a sector strategy established under his predecessor, David Dinkins. At the heart of the sector strategy was the formation of groups comprising business owners, labor representatives, academics, and nonprofit professionals to sit at the table with city officials to identify and remove barriers to growth in their industries.

Giuliani, who preferred to criticize Dinkins and what he called "the old way of thinking," had none of it. As Giuliani eagerly gave tax abatements to major finance and media firms that threatened to move, he undercut New York's middle class with land-use priorities (such as those favoring big-box stores) that chased good manufacturing jobs out of the city at a far faster rate than necessary. Indeed, the city lost fully 30 percent of its manufacturing employment during the 1990s, while seven of the nation's ten largest cities either gained or maintained steady manufacturing employment.

Though economic development wasn't high on Giuliani's political agenda, he was ever eager to take credit for economic growth. The redevelopment of Times Square was just one example where he sought to rewrite the history of the once-seedy district's transformation. Times Square's changes were initiated under former Mayor Edward Koch. One of the most catalytic deals—with Disney—was worked out under Dinkins.

Even after this redevelopment was well afoot, Giuliani did not even try to ensure that the jobs that emerged in hotels, restaurants, and other aspects of the enlivened hospitality trade were good jobs. In Las Vegas, labor, management, and government partnership help make certain that hospitality jobs provided middle-class wages, career ladders, and health benefits. New York's tourism jobs continued in many instances to be low-wage, even dead-end, positions, with the exception of slots in the largely unionized hotel sector and those at the handful of unionized restaurants. While Giuliani trumpeted a reduction of the hotel tax as an important spark to an increased hotel occupancy rate, the spurt in activity had begun before the surcharge on patrons' hotel bills was expunged. And, in the wake of the tax cut, hotels raised prices promptly by an amount that exceeded the margin of the tax reduction. Hotel owners, not customers, were the beneficiaries.

* * *

When it came to setting the government's fiscal policy, Giuliani followed a pattern of irresponsibility that is becoming increasingly common among some conservatives nationally. On the one hand, Giuliani increased the city's long-term debt; on the other, he tightly constrained the city's ability to repay the debt. Between the first budget he inherited and his final year's budget, he increased the city's outstanding debt by nearly 50 percent, drawing justifiable criticism from both conservative and liberal budget watchdog groups. The mayor could have covered more of the city's capital costs using the increased revenues during the surplus years. Instead he continued to cut taxes and step up long-range borrowing. The tax cuts, primarily for businesses, cost the city's government an average of $2.5 billion a year in revenue. That is roughly the same amount of money raised by the 18.49 percent increase in the property tax that Bloomberg instituted in the middle of 2003. The Bloomberg tax increase was clearly a legacy of Giuliani's stunning profligacy—a stewardship at odds with the prudent image the mayor preferred to project.

At the same time, importantly, the mayor didn't fare well in Albany; his go-it-alone style proved disastrous as a mode of operating in a capital where the slow cultivation of favor is the preferred path to an eventual back-room deal. New York City paid a price for Giuliani's unwillingness to curry favor with Albany's powerful "three men in a room"—Governor George Pataki, State Senate majority leader Joseph Bruno, and State Assembly speaker Sheldon Silver.

Indeed, on Giuliani's watch the New York State legislature eliminated the fractional "commuter tax" on nonresidents who worked in the city, depriving the city's coffers of what had been a reliable revenue stream worth up to $500 million a year. Giuliani howled in protest, but the deal was done, with a pivotal role having been played by Silver, a New York City Democrat with whom Giuliani had gained little influence.

The mayor fought ineffectively, too, for an increase in the rent the city received from the Port Authority of New York and New

Jersey for the public land on which La Guardia and John F. Kennedy airports sit; the more businesslike Bloomberg was able to work out both an increase in rent and several hundred million in back rent with the governors who control the mammoth bi-state authority. In much the same way, Bloomberg won direct control over the New York City schools, something deeply coveted by Giuliani.

Giuliani's notions about the city's finances also undermined the fiscal foundations of the city's subway system, so vital to New York's economic vitality. He reduced by $90 million the city's annual transit subsidy that allowed children to take buses and subways to school without charge, expecting (correctly) that the state's Metropolitan Transportation Authority would pick up the expense rather than making kids start paying their own way. While this saved the city $90 million, it also opened the way, politically, for the governor to reduce the state's contributions to the transit system. The MTA had to increase its borrowing, dip into the fare box to cover the debt, and eventually raise fares.

It would be inaccurate to say Giuliani made no contributions to economic growth. His focus on public safety and quality of life helped improve the reputation—and the reality—of life in many neighborhoods. Though he may have claimed more credit than he deserved—crime began falling during the last half of the Dinkins years—he brought national attention to the sharp drop in crime and encouraged people to move to and invest in the city.

In addition, while other members of his political party blamed immigration for weak spots in the economy and in particular the low-wage labor market, Giuliani never did, properly recognizing immigrants as an important component of economic growth.

On balance, however, Giuliani squandered one of New York City's best opportunities to make the local economy less unequal, to gain middle-class jobs and to reduce the crushing burden of long-term debt. He instead surfed the go-go nineties, serving up tax cuts and borrowing extravagantly. By the end of his time at City Hall, when the Wall Street–driven economy began to slump, the mayor had done nothing to prepare the city for the tumble.

For the biggest trick in managing New York's volatile economy during boom times, by a long shot, isn't keeping stock prices soaring or real estate prices flying high in the sky. Rather, it's making sure that the benefits are spread as widely as possible, that the city's economic base grows more diversified, and that the government's fiscal condition is cushioned for a stock-market downturn. Rudy Giuliani, for his part, left office with most New Yorkers no better off because of the boom and the city unprepared for the bust.

9

Budget
Paul Moses

Rudy Giuliani bounded over to my desk in the pressroom of the federal courthouse in Manhattan, handcuffed me, looked me in the eyes, and read me my rights. It was November 1984, and Giuliani had begun to make a name for himself after a year and a half as the U.S. attorney in Manhattan. Already, early in his public career, he was accustomed to winning. And now he was about to turn the tables by playing a joke on a young reporter who had poked fun at him.

As part of the festivities for my last day of work as a reporter for the Associated Press, I had drafted a mock indictment and press release in which Giuliani charged the courthouse press corps with an anti-trust conspiracy to avoid publicizing his great achievements to the extent they deserved. The indictment exaggerated all of those accomplishments, and the press release further exaggerated what was in the indictment. I thought it was a pretty clever spoof of Giuliani, since the courthouse press corps knew all too well his enormous appetite for publicity and his penchant for hype. But I wasn't so sure it was a good idea for a visiting reporter from the *Washington Post* to bring the fake documents over to Giuliani's office. The up-and-coming prosecutor took it in good humor, returning the favor by clasping the cuffs on me a tad beyond snug.

The pressroom prank I cooked up reminds me that long before Giuliani was mythologized as "America's Mayor," I had spotted in him a particular drive for self-promotion and an instinct for exaggeration. After my stint with the Associated Press, I returned to cover Giuliani in federal court and later in City Hall for *Newsday*, watching as he created a compelling narrative in which he starred as the man who turned around the nation's largest city. As in my bogus press release, key parts of that story were exaggerated.

That's the case for his record in managing New York City's finances, which, along with crime fighting, serves as a cornerstone of Giuliani's self-narrative. As with many a myth, the story begins in the bad old days and is wrapped around a kernel of truth: the demons of liberal fiscal mismanagement bedeviled New York City. For thirty years before Giuliani took office, the "old philosophy," as he put it, was to increase spending year in and year out. No one worried about long-term consequences. But, as Giuliani said of his own administration in a 1997 speech, "We have looked at the budget in a different way. We now understand that every choice we make has not only an effect on this year's calculations, but on the very future of the city five, ten, and fifteen years down the road." Our hero cast himself as the first fiscally responsible mayor of the city in decades, one who charted a bold new course by cutting spending and reducing the size of government. He also battled against the notion that cutting taxes reduced a city's revenues.

At the end of his first term, when Giuliani gave that speech, he could legitimately claim to have disciplined New York's wayward budget. He accomplished the rare feat of cutting spending in his first year, and it hardly budged for two years after that, staying well below the inflation rate. But in his second term his handling of city finances was far different. According to a city comptroller report, Giuliani increased city spending at three times the rate of inflation during those years. And when it is all averaged out and adjusted for inflation, the numbers show that Giuliani was a bigger spender than Mayor David Dinkins, the Democrat who Giuliani scorned as an icon of the bad old days of liberal profligacy.

To put it in budget-speak: Spending of locally raised revenue increased at more than one and a half times the rate of inflation when averaged out over the seven budgets that fell fully within Giuliani's two terms. It increased at slightly *less* for the three budgets entirely on Dinkins's watch. (The city budget year begins on July 1.)

No one ever said it was easy to manage New York City's budget. By 2001, it had reached more than $40 billion annually, with about 70 percent of that sum raised directly by city taxes and fees (the rest comes mostly from state and federal grants). It's the fifth largest government budget in the country, following the federal government and the states of California, New York, and Texas. Giuliani was right to say that any decisions he made would affect "the very future of the city" for years down the road—and probably the sprawling metropolitan region as well. But weeks after giving that speech, Giuliani proposed an election-year budget that would ultimately increase city-funded spending 6 percent, or nearly four times the rate of inflation—anathema for any true fiscal conservative. He also continued to cut taxes, a choice that seemed attractive at the time but which would later put the city in a fiscal hole because spending was not similarly cut.

Giuliani, who claimed that each budget he introduced decreased spending, increased spending in all but one of his budgets. He incurred huge new costs for politically helpful projects, such as closing a landfill on Staten Island without having a real plan for disposing the city's trash. He created much greater gaps in future budgets by cutting $2.5 billion in annual taxes, even as he scorned the many experts who warned his policies would damage the city in the future. He further compromised future budgets by granting tax breaks for real estate projects that would have been built without a city subsidy. And he left his successor, Michael Bloomberg, with a fiscal crisis—in many ways the worst since the city's brush with near-bankruptcy in the bad old 1970s—that could be resolved only by raising taxes.

In the end, Giuliani did what other mayors have done since the city crawled back from its mid-1970s fiscal crisis: he balanced budgets under sometimes painful circumstances and used the slack to fund his immediate political priorities. For Giuliani, who planned to run for higher office as a crime-fighter and tax-cutter, that meant funding tax cuts and a larger police force. Despite his rhetoric, Giuliani failed to take advantage of the flush city economy during the Wall Street boom years in the late 1990s to solve the city's long-term budget problem—the "structural gap" in which expenses continually rose faster than revenues, creating recurring deficits year after year. He used surpluses to protect against any shortfalls during his own mayoralty but not to reduce mounting debt in the long term. That's not to say he was a terrible fiscal manager; other politicians in his position might have raised spending more than he did during the boom years. But he was no model.

In one sense, he was like his White House hero, President Ronald Reagan, who cut taxes while increasing spending on defense, leaving his successor, President George H.W. Bush, such a depleted budget that Bush was forced to violate a campaign pledge and raise taxes. Reagan became the stuff of legend, at least in conservative circles. Giuliani became a legend, too: "America's Mayor." Meanwhile, Bush I and Bloomberg were derided.

* * *

If this was just a matter of determining which politicians should be enshrined in public opinion, it wouldn't be that important. The real is issue is this: Before Giuliani, public opinion in New York and many other big cities generally accepted the "old way," the view that there was an undeniable link between a city's spending and the basic services it could afford to provide. It was accepted that any cut in spending would often mean dirtier streets, fewer police officers, or larger class sizes. New Yorkers had learned that the hard way—the city had skidded and nearly crashed after thousands of workers were laid off to avert bankruptcy in 1975.

But Giuliani, through hype and repetition, convinced many New Yorkers, including influential segments of the news media, that with business-like management, it was possible to spend less and at the same time enhance public services. He may have been so persuasive to many simply because, in reality, he spent more of the taxpayers' money to fund public services while he was claiming to spend less. Similarly, he increased, rather than shrank, the city's workforce. And he accomplished that sleight-of-hand while reaping the political benefits of cutting local taxes.

Giuliani was so persuasive a mythmaker that New Yorkers reelected him by a huge margin in 1997 and went on to choose Bloomberg, his candidate, to continue his business-like philosophy of governing. But Bloomberg, the real-life businessman, quickly contradicted him. He was dismayed at how much money the city had given away in dubious tax breaks for big companies and called for an end to "corporate welfare." He didn't view government as some bloated blob that could be cut indefinitely to save money; rather, he found it relatively efficient. Sensibly, he found that it was better to raise property taxes than to cut services too much, which would drive away people who wanted to live or do business in the city. He was met with a tide of anger.

"Mayor Mike likes big government: From Day One, he's bent over backward to spare every last dollar of spending," the *New York Post* editorialized.

The difficulty Bloomberg faced was that he could not compete with a myth. In the year that ended June 30, 2001, the last full budget year under Giuliani's mayoralty, city-funded spending increased more than 9 percent, according to the Independent Budget Office, a nonpartisan city agency akin to the Congressional Budget Office. That was far more than any spending increase under Dinkins, and nearly quadruple the rate of the Bloomberg spending increase the *Post* was complaining about.

Similarly, Bloomberg reduced the number of city employees to well below the level Giuliani left him. Giuliani credits himself with reducing the size of government, claiming in his book *Leadership* that "the city payroll was reduced by more than 20,000 employees" during his administration. Again, there is exaggeration. The total number of city employees increased slightly during his mayoralty. But thanks in part to increased federal aid, the number of full-time jobs funded with city money fell by close to 3 percent, about eight thousand jobs. The catch was that spending on part-time employment grew seven-fold during Giuliani's administration as the city agencies whose budgets he restrained struggled to maintain services, according to a study by the Independent Budget Office. The study estimated the number of "full-time equivalent" employees, or FTEs, and found that city employment increased 4 percent from 1991, during the Dinkins administration, to the end of 2001, when Giuliani left office.

Giuliani's bestselling book contains the misleading claim that the average annual rate of spending increases grew less on his watch than in the past. It's misleading because he doesn't account for the rate of inflation. In Giuliani's second term, as he planned to run for the U.S. Senate against Hillary Rodham Clinton, city-funded spending grew more than $1 billion a year, an average increase of 6 percent each year, according to figures from the Independent Budget Office. Perhaps that should be expected, since the stock market was booming and the city had plenty of money. The real manipulation, though, was that every year, Giuliani would claim that his new budget for the following year would reduce spending. "Year-To-Year Spending Reduced By 2%," he announced in unveiling his budget for 2001. The budget actually increased year-to-year spending by 9 percent, more than three and a half times the New York–area inflation rate. He repeated this bogus message over and over. "The cornerstone of this success has been our ability to control the growth of spending," he wrote in his newspaper column, which was printed in many neighborhood papers. ". . . This is a time to strengthen our City's fiscal position, not to return to the undisciplined, high-spending policies of the past."

Giuliani did precisely that in his second term, but obscured the spending increases with an accounting device. Because the boom on Wall Street created multi-billion-dollar surpluses in his second term, a reserve fund could be carried over from one year to the next, where it helped to fill the gigantic budget gaps that routinely plague New York's mayors. The spending was listed to the *previous* year rather than to the new budget, giving the illusion that the new budget's spending was being slashed. Some fiscal observers urged that, instead of using this reserve fund to pre-pay interest on the following year's capital debt, the mayor should use the surplus to pay the city's long-term capital debt. That move would have saved money in the long run and significantly eased the burden for future mayors.

Instead, Giuliani spent. Some of the increased spending went to the school system, which Giuliani had attacked constantly for waste during his first term. After a while, it became clear that these attacks had produced a major political problem for him. Whenever education topped the list of voters' concerns, polls showed that his standing dropped perilously. It became clear by the end of Giuliani's first term that his refusal to provide enough money for school construction had worsened the severe overcrowding in public schools. So he reversed himself. "Proposes Largest Capital Budget in History for Board of Education," read the headline on the press release for his 2001 budget. Although the city still shortchanged its schools, Giuliani created a conventional wisdom that said New York City spent generously on education.

The truth was quite the opposite. When a State Supreme Court justice ruled in 2001 that New York State systematically short-changed the city's public school students with an unfair and racially biased school-aid formula, he also noted that the city underfunded its own students as well—communities in the rest of the state spent much more per pupil. The judge noted that the city had cut taxes repeatedly even as its students got an illegally below-standard education—overcrowded classes, crumbling facilities, poorly paid and unqualified teachers—because of the shortage of school funding. (The ruling was upheld by the state's highest court, the Court of Appeals.)

Giuliani shouldn't be faulted for spending more on schools—it was necessary, just as it was necessary for David Dinkins to spend more money to hire police in the midst of a crime wave. But Giuliani's claim to have reversed the free-spending ways of New York's past is simply false.

The fat years gave Giuliani a unique chance to resolve the city's longstanding budget gaps, which persisted because spending constantly sped ahead of revenues. In practical terms, this "structural" gap means that far into the future, each mayor can expect to face a multi-billion-dollar chasm in the budget. Since the city must by law have a balanced budget, the city government faces wrenching political choices year after year that pit important services against each other.

If anything, Giuliani made the task tougher for his successors through a dangerous combination of lowering taxes and increasing spending. His tax cuts, largely made possible by a temporary bubble in the economy, extracted $2.5 billion a year from the budget. Once the economy cooled off, that left an immense hole that had to be filled if the city was going to maintain vital services.

Tax cuts should be a goal for New York City, considering its heavy taxation. But Giuliani continued to cut taxes in 2001 as the economy headed into a downturn—even as he hiked spending at more than triple the rate of inflation. Following in Reagan's footsteps, he promoted the idea that tax cuts would pay for themselves by heating up the economy.

"Even though it seems in the short run that cutting taxes means less money for government, and makes it harder to reduce our deficits, time and again we've proven that just the opposite is true," Giuliani said in 1997.

The billboard for that argument was a small cut Giuliani made in 1994 in the tax on hotel rooms. The combined state and local tax on hotel occupancy had increased from 15.25 percent in 1990 to 21.25 percent—the highest in the country—by the time he took office in 1994. In some ways, it was an easy tax to increase, since local voters didn't pay it. Giuliani argued when he ran for mayor that reducing the hotel tax would increase tourism. In 1994 the state knocked five percentage points off the tax, and the city reduced its take by one point.

"The result has been a boon for our tourism industry, our convention centers, and hotels," Giuliani said, going on to explain that the city collected more money from the lower tax.

Giuliani cited the example tirelessly, saying it showed that selected tax cuts would pay for themselves. But a 1997 study by the city's Independent Budget Office found that even in the case of the hotel tax—a very specific and outrageously high levy—the tax cut fell short of paying for itself by half. The study noted that the reduced tax was just one in a number of factors responsible for the rise in hotel occupancy. In fact, it said, hotel rooms had begun filling up and rates had started rising even before the tax was cut.

The study didn't say it was a bad idea to reduce the tax. But it exposed a Giuliani method of operation: he had taken a solid accomplishment and exaggerated it, elevating a good idea to the level of wizardry. Giuliani continued to cite the hotel tax as he cut twenty-two more city taxes during his mayoralty.

When other public officials sought to initiate and get credit for tax cuts, Giuliani charged them with being irresponsible. In 1998,

Council Speaker Peter Vallone, then running an ultimately unsuccessful campaign as the Democratic nominee for governor, took control of the city budget process and passed a plan over Giuliani's veto that raised spending and eliminated an income-tax surcharge.

"If you want to reduce taxes and be a hero for reducing taxes, then you've got to reduce spending," Giuliani, in a twist, suddenly retorted—this, at a time when he was finishing up a budget year in which city-funded spending increased at nearly four times the rate of inflation. He complained that the City Council "would like the best of both worlds."

Similarly, Giuliani blasted state legislators who voted to eliminate a tax on suburban commuters that had brought $500 million a year into city coffers. He was right to condemn them, but he was responsible for the atmosphere that made it happen. He had touted his own tax cuts so loudly and successfully that other public officials wanted to claim their own glory. After all, he had argued over and over that the city not only could afford to cut taxes but also gained from it.

But the city couldn't afford it. Well before the World Trade Center fell, fiscal monitors warned that the combination of multiple tax cuts, rising debt, and increased spending could devastate city finances in the long run. Then the economy started to turn down, and the terrorist attack further jolted it.

After eight years of Giuliani's mayoralty, New Yorkers still looked ahead to budgets with multi-billion-dollar deficits and to all the worries that entails, from finding money to rebuild schools and maintain the subway fare to having enough workers to pick up the trash. Many New Yorkers turned on the new mayor when he raised property taxes—so unlike Giuliani—but he had little choice.

He, too, had been handcuffed.

Order
Luc Sante

YOU REALLY COULDN'T hope to find a better illustration of Rudolph Giuliani's terms as mayor of New York City than his stance on jaywalking. The practice of crossing the street against traffic or when the light is red or in the middle of the block is probably the single most common form of law-breaking, especially now that littering has become deeply unfashionable, and spitting on the sidewalk has virtually disappeared. Laws prohibiting jaywalking are universally understood to symbolize a city's parental stance toward its infantile citizens; in cities around the world they are primarily a cheap and easy way for a beat cop to meet his daily ticket quota. New York City, however, might as well be the capital of jaywalking—it could call itself the City of Jaywalkers. It is the inverse of those German cities in which travelers are astonished to find crowds of pedestrians waiting placidly for the light to change even when there is no traffic to be seen for miles in either direction. Jaywalking is a New Yorker's birthright, a minor but indispensable sign of his or her independence and self-sufficiency. New Yorkers can cross anywhere at any time if they need to, and if they get themselves creamed, they accept that it will be their own damn fault. It is their city, after all, not one lent to them on a merit basis by cops or bureaucrats.

The fact that Giuliani chose to have his police officers aggressively enforce the anti-jaywalking statutes was a flung gauntlet, a proclamation that he intended to remake the city in his own image for his own pleasure. Unlike most mayors, he would not be adapting himself to better serve his city, but would be adapting the city for it to serve him. Not being one for half-measures, he then raised the ante far beyond anyone's speculations by declaring certain formerly legal street-crossings off-limits—installing fences on Midtown corners to prevent any pedestrian traffic at those points, so as not to impede the flow of motor vehicles on the major arteries. Favoring cars over people flew in the face of most current urbanist thinking, went directly against the trend of cities, such as London and Amsterdam, that had been doing their best to reduce vehicular traffic in their centers—but Giuliani's actions had far less to do with traffic control than with behavior modification. He was determined to rule over an obedient citizenry. He would effect a personality change in New Yorkers by forcing them to adhere to whimsical and arbitrary mandates.

The enforcement of the statutes on jaywalking was perhaps thinly justified by the "broken windows" theory, a voguish neoliberal construct that held that the number of minor infractions observed in a district—graffiti, panhandlers, subway-fare evasions—was proportional to the amount of significant crimes, of murders, rapes, and felonious assaults. You might as well say that the number of dust bunnies observed under furniture was somehow predictive of the chances that the house would burn down, but it was hardly coincidental that most such "lifestyle crimes"—jaywalking was a notable exception—were largely limited to, and taken for granted by, the poor. In previous decades there had been rashes of enforcement of particular infractions, notably graffiti, which was the focus of a virulent media campaign that just happened to coincide with its flowering as an art form, but most such torts had traditionally been engrained in city life. Begging, for example, went back to the prehistory of cities, and even conservative regimes had long been inclined to view it as an occasion for demonstrative charity, if not as a reproach to materialist self-satisfaction. Unlicensed sidewalk vending of secondhand goods had flourished in the poorer neighborhoods of New York more or less forever, but under the mayoral administration of Ed Koch the police had begun to harass vendors on the pretext that their goods might have been stolen property. Under Giuliani, the enforcement of such petty laws became draconian and unavoidable, and the number of targetable infractions swelled dramatically. Out-of-towners who desired a quick nutshell view of the city's tone in those years would be taken to the Criminal Courts Building on Monday morning, to observe the endless line of otherwise blameless citizens who had been given a bench-appearance ticket over the weekend for drinking beer—concealed by paper bags—on the sidewalk.

New York City was hardly alone in its attempts to erase these aspects of its fabric that journalists tended to characterize with the adjective "gritty." It was the era when gentrification went into overdrive, and hardly any urban neighborhood, no matter how ill-constructed and godforsaken, was safe from the incursion of smart boutiques and chic restaurants—businesses that were only affordable for the well-to-do. New York's transformation differed in the pedantic obsessiveness with which laws were combed to find a basis for extirpating all manifestations of street life, and the harshly punitive way in which those sweeps were carried out. Those items carried Giuliani's signature. He had first made his name as a prosecutor whose ruthless zeal for conviction suggested some throwback hybrid of Thomas E. Dewey and J. Edgar Hoover. It may have been the late author and columnist Murray Kempton who applied to him Carlyle's characterization of Robespierre: "a sea-green incorruptible." He set the tone of his mayoral administration very early, with a speech given at a forum on city crime in which he asserted that "Freedom is about authority. Freedom is about the willingness of every single human being to cede to lawful authority a great deal of discretion about what you do and how you do it." That speech struck me as uncomfortably reminiscent of some statements that had been made sixty-odd years earlier. For example, "State and individual are identical, and the art of government is the art of so reconciling and uniting the two terms that a maximum of liberty harmonizes with a maximum of public order. . . . For the maximum liberty always coincides with the maximum force of the state." Those words were written by Giovanni Gentile, the official philosopher of Fascism under Mussolini. Few made the connection in print, just as only a few publicly noted the then-mayor's philosophical debt to Girolamo Savonarola, the scold of fifteenth-century Florence, because of an unwillingness to appear in thrall to an ethnic stereotype.

Giuliani was tireless. He bullied, hectored, and sought to marginalize anyone who dared oppose him. No sooner had one battle been joined than he opened another front, so that he could ensure the dispersal of outrage. The mayoral podium seemed to be erected in five or six places per day for the benefit of the evening news, and it became exhausting trying to take in all his various but singularly pointed performances. He would be refusing to apologize for the unjustifiable murder of a black man by the police over here, then attempting to abrogate freedom of expression over there, then arguing for tax exemptions for the very rich somewhere else. He long succeeded in outshouting and outrunning the opposition, and coasted in popular esteem on the pretense that he single-handedly lowered the crime rate.

By 2001, however, his public image was somewhat battered, the greatest harm having come to it from his long-running divorce battle rather than from any graver matter. Just when it looked as though he might have lost the support of the city and would be forced to slink from office at the close of his term, he was delivered by a *deus ex machina*: 9/11. He played the part of embattled leader well—the enormity at hand being sufficient to make his choleric personality seem reasonable by contrast. No one had ever suggested that Giuliani was unintelligent or ill-prepared, and he demonstrated his competence quite conspicuously, even allowing a reporter to witness him consulting a biography of Winston Churchill. In the end, however, a letter to the *Village Voice*, published later that September, summarized matters rather tersely. Giuliani is forever being credited (I am quoting from memory) with "rising to the occasion," the writer noted, but the truth is that the horror of 9/11 has dragged the city down to his level.

Giuliani is in an excellent position at present. His consulting firm is hired by cities around the world that seek hints on how to make their intransigent underclasses and surviving dissident fringes disappear from sight. He is favored by the Republican Party as an aggressive speaker and militant presence who has had combat experience; as an operative who might have retained credibility in the traditionally liberal urban enclaves as a man who has gay friends and has been known to read a book. Meanwhile, he has left a New York City that has had much of its identity bled from it. It is a city of chain franchises and million-dollar hovels, of minimized public services and sweetheart tax deals, of a corporate Times Square and a whitened Harlem. There is less discourse and exchange across class lines than there has ever been, and whatever life and vigor and color the city retains has a great deal to do with Giuliani's inability to entirely vacate the rent-stabilization laws. The city he has left might in a generation or two be interchangeable with Phoenix or Atlanta, but for some geographic quirks. It should be noted, however, that the trains have already ceased to run on time.

Liberty
Debbie Nathan

I MOVED FROM Texas to New York City shortly before 9/11. The day afterward, a friend from San Antonio phoned to see if I was okay and to comfort me. I had to lower the sound on the television to hear him guffaw, "Guess what the mayor did here? He shut down the Tower of the Americas—said the terrorists might bomb it!" I chuckled, too, as my own mayor, Giuliani, intoned in the background.

The joke was the conceit of thinking that anyone interested in attacking the United States would bother with a nothing place like San Antonio. The Tower of the Americas has been inaccurately compared to the Washington Monument. While the two landmarks are about the same height, the San Antonio landmark has nowhere near the same degree of streamlined grace. It has a giant needle at the top along with a squat, disc-like restaurant that serves bland and overpriced food to tourists—all supported by an overly tall column that looks like a Greek temple fragment on steroids. It was built in 1968 for an exposition called HemisFair, which was sanctioned by the international World's Fair and constructed with hoopla by boosters of the South Texas economy. A generation later, the edifice seems like something out of the Jetsons. To imagine a terrorist cathecting it as a symbol of American hubris is ludicrous.

My friend got me to laugh, but through the giggles there was still the sight of Rudolph Giuliani in my Manhattan living room, dispensing order and calm. And not just to New Yorkers. This was national television and people in San Antonio and countless other burgs were listening to Giuliani now—just as he'd been listening, for some years prior, to them. Specifically, he listened to their fears about big-city disorder—the kind begotten by those people who complain aggressively about poverty and prejudice, those people with wooly thoughts and megaphones to shout them through, people making and displaying blasphemous art, people hawking all manner of goods on the street.

Such people are just not well liked in most American cities, especially in those cities with leaders who have promoted economic development schemes based on tourism. Rabble and rabble-rousers scare visitors, the thinking goes, and even strip clubs are threats, now that conventioneers are routinely urged to bring the wife and kids along for the business trip. San Antonio thus beckons with its Six Flags, Sea World, and the River Walk—a downtown Spanish-colonial fantasy stroll clogged with out-of-towners and incongruously graced with tropical foliage, motorboats, mariachi bands, chain luxury hotels, and nouvelle tamales. It wasn't always so kitschy. The riverbank was only lightly developed, and sparsely visited, until HemisFair came along—the result of the city's more visionary fathers' decision to gussy up the city's Mexicanness (some 60 percent of the population is Latino) and market it predominantly to white out-of-towners.

San Antonio has become one of the country's most popular tourist destinations, so orderly that it feels un-citylike and insufferable (which is why I moved to New York). When I lived in San Antonio and was unsuccessfully trying to get used to the place in the late 1990s, the police in one affluent neighborhood had taken to fining teens caught smoking cigarettes in their own yards. Downtown, meanwhile, the policy was to clear the area of suspected gang members. In practice, this meant harassing Hispanic adolescents with their baseball caps on backward who had strayed onto the River Walk from their crumbling neighborhoods blocks away.

Remarkably, although old postcards of the city document a lively tradition of street vending, there was virtually nothing for sale under the sun. Now, everything was either in malls or "El Mercado," a municipal market that looked like a south-of-the-border pueblo reinterpreted for Disney World. (I once heard a tourist rave about El Mercado for being "just like Mexico but better because it's clean.")

Free expression was also sanitized, with hardly a raised eyebrow from the community. Without a whit of public complaint from its patrons, the public library system opened a branch where patrons had to sign a registry to enter. The reason for this security: the branch was in the library of a high school. That meant adults couldn't use it until evening (so as to shield students from those who could do them harm, say, pedophiles). It also meant that books deemed inappropriate for the high school library (books explaining abortion and how to get one, for example) were not available to grown-ups, either. Likewise, the branch's Internet was filtered to protect patrons of all ages from pornographic images.

The city said it had to put the library in the high school because of budget constraints. But fiscal responsibility was also cited as the rationale for creating a situation that closely resembled the Brooklyn Museum freedom-of-expression debacle in October 1999 under Giuliani. San Antonio annually gives money to arts groups and is particularly receptive to those that promote cheery activities such as piñata making. When, in 1997, Esperanza Center, a group of leftist, feminist women who organized cultural events in the Hispanic community, launched an "Out at the Movies" series featuring films that dealt with gay and lesbian themes, right-wing Christian groups were outraged. Many stormed City Hall, and soon Esperanza's funding was cut to zero. The group's programming was too political for the mayor and San Antonio City Council. And besides, some officials said, arts funds should be reserved for art that spurs tourism.

Was Giuliani aware of the "Out at the Movies" brouhaha when he moved to de-fund the Brooklyn Museum in late 1999 because of its Sensation exhibit, which he deemed anti-Catholic and "sick?" Probably not. But it was similarly out of sync with his cleaned-up vision for Gotham, not to mention his goal of defeating Hillary Rodham Clinton in the U.S. Senate race that year with the help of the large number of Catholic voters upstate.

Kurt Vonnegut once described the illusion that New York City gives to almost anybody—"that he must be accomplishing something by talking or eating or drinking or reading a newspaper in such a busy, expensive place." By the time the Brooklyn Museum was threatened with a City Hall–inspired shutdown, the concept was associated in the national mind with upscale chain stores, private memberships, and, if not unremitting politesse, then disapproval of petty annoyances limited to cute, faux-Jewish wisecracking à la *Seinfeld* (a popular show around San Antonio).

What viewers there didn't see on the sitcom, and perhaps didn't want to see, were representations of poverty, racial tension, and class conflict that were also part of the character of New York. By the early 1990s, the city was rebounding from the chronic budget shortfalls of the previous two decades. But the municipal government's return to the black was grounded in finance and real estate speculation that only deepened economic inequality. In Manhattan, the richest 20 percent of the population (the one perhaps including Jerry, George, and Elaine) had a median income that was thirty-two times higher than the poorest 20 percent. The gap, reported the *New York Times* in 1994, was surpassed in the United States "only by a group of 70 households near a former leper colony in Hawaii." The *Times* also noted that poor people across the entire New York metropolitan region were more heavily concentrated inside the boundaries of the city than they were in any other metropolitan area except San Antonio.

This state of affairs promised to worsen in 1994, when Newt Gingrich unveiled his Contract for America, including major federal funding cuts for cities. New York State in a sense signed onto Gingrich's urban policy that year by electing conservative Republican George Pataki as governor. Giuliani, for his part, would have to work assiduously to live down his endorsement of the liberal Democratic incumbent, Mario Cuomo, yoking his future political ambitions increasingly to the GOP. After winning re-election to his second and last allowable term as mayor in heavily Democratic New York, he started running down the city, speaking of it as bonded to perverse notions and habits wrought by years of liberal mismanagement.

"It would be a good thing," Giuliani would say early in his tenure, for the poor to achieve "mobility"—out of the city. New York, he seemed to suggest, could be more hostile to the indigent and more hospitable to the monied. This was not a new suggestion.

In 1987, during Edward Koch's mayoralty, the urbanist Marshall Berman had interpreted City Hall's goals as seeking to transform the city "into a place where capital from anywhere in the world is instantly at home, while everybody without capital is increasingly out of place."

* * *

Those instantly at home in Giuliani's New York included people who could afford $100 Broadway tickets, $250-a-night hotel rooms, and if they decided to relocate to the city, upward of $2,000-a-month in rent for claustrophobic apartments in Soho or Park Slope. Among the newly devalued were health activists who wanted to distribute clean needles to heroin users in parks to stem HIV infection; immigrant taxi drivers less interested in dispensing quaint wisdom to passengers than in protesting draconian, Giuliani-imposed rules of conduct by driving en masse over the Triboro Bridge; advocates for the poor who disagreed with the city's tight-fisted welfare policies and wished to communicate their opposition outside Gracie Mansion or City Hall; Socialist Workers Party stalwarts handing out leaflets; union rank and file members picketing for raises; members of a black-nationalist religious sect whose loud proselytizing in Times Square included racist denunciations of whites and Jews. And there were those art vendors on the sidewalks in front of museums and in nice parks, hawking paintings and sculptures that galleries weren't interested in. In the Giuliani era, all were needless clutter or, even worse, springboards to disobedience and disorder.

Even prior to Giuliani's mayoralty, Business Improvement District mavens and economic developers disliked the noisy and reproachful style of these old-school New Yorkers. David Dinkins was still mayor when street vendors of non-art ephemera, such as Senegalese immigrants selling watches and sunglasses, were forbidden to ply their trade in fashionable Manhattan districts. But when Giuliani took office, it was time to get control of everyone: to deny permits, make arrests, or both.

Curiously, art was an early target: From 1993 to 1996, over four hundred painters, sculptors, photographers, and printmakers were arrested and their wares seized and destroyed. Some of the busts stopped after an appeals court ruled that art vendors had a right to sell on the sidewalks. But another arrest and confiscation wave had started in 1995, when the Giuliani administration declared that only fifty-one vendors could sell near the Metropolitan Museum and in other tourist-infused areas of the city's park system; those fifty-one would be chosen by a lottery and receive licenses, and anyone vending without one would be considered a lawbreaker.

Such policies inspired legal challenges based on First Amendment arguments that were legion during the Giuliani years. As time went on, the administration's attempts to stifle what we call "free speech" became more frequent, more obvious, and more obnoxious to New Yorkers. By the time the mayor left office, the city had litigated—unsuccessfully in nearly every case—over two dozen free speech challenges, more than under any previous administration.

Early on, many New Yorkers, tested by a long national recession, a high crime rate and a crack epidemic, applauded Giuliani's clampdowns. Plenty bought into his embrace of the "broken windows" theory that crime goes down and property values and tourism grow when petty disorder (such as shattered glass) is nipped in the bud. If nipping meant clearing high-end public spaces of starving artists, peep shows, and ranting Black Israelites, so be it. But when the city also started attacking art and political expression that out-of-towners might find offensive—under the rubric of fostering a better quality of life for all—many New Yorkers grew uneasy. It was, after all, the fundamental and enshrined right of every New Yorker to be left alone and say whatever is on his or her mind. While one might buy into sweeping panhandlers off the streets and subways, it was quite another thing to tolerate the mayor's unparalleled restrictions on demonstrations on the steps of City Hall or dancing in bars.

The use of such tactics only grew after Giuliani won his second term with a landslide, sixteen-point victory over Democrat Ruth Messinger. The victory induced a mania (albeit forced) among his staff about the chances of his going national—of the mayor running for president as early as 2000 as a Republican. To compete with the likes of William Bennett, Lamar Alexander, and Pat Buchanan, he would have to play to a conservative audience, and he did this, in part, by noisily thrashing the First Amendment.

Late that year, a group of pagans on Staten Island were forbidden by the city from gathering on a beach to celebrate winter Solstice, a move that attracted attention within and beyond this predominantly Republican borough. But Spencer Tunick's application for a permit to stage a photo shoot in Manhattan did get some statewide and national press. Tunick, who is renowned for posing dozens of people nude outdoors in abstract patterns, asked the city for permission to hold this particular shoot at dawn, when few passersby or vehicles would be around. As many a Broadway hit attests, public nudity in New York City is allowed in artistic performances: theoretically, a naked presentation of *Hamlet* could be legally staged in Grand Central Station. Nevertheless, the city denied Tunick's request.

When Giuliani first saw the catalog for the Brooklyn Museum's Sensation exhibit in the fall of 1999, the administration's commissioner of cultural affairs, Schuyler Chapin, had already reviewed and approved the contents. By now, the mayor had mothballed his presidential ambitions and decided to run against Hillary Rodham Clinton for the Senate seat that Daniel Patrick Moynihan was vacating in order to retire. Upstate New York being heavily Catholic, Giuliani made an issue of "The Holy Virgin Mary," a Sensation painting that used, among other materials, elephant dung to depict the mother of Christ. "The Catholic League will go after it; Cardinal O'Connor and the Catholics will go crazy," supposedly advised his press secretary, according to *The Full Rudy*, a book by a veteran New York journalist, the late Jack Newfield. The mayor promptly denounced the exhibit as hate speech against Catholics and vowed to defund and close down the museum. The museum, of course, immediately sued on First Amendment grounds identical to those used by Esperanza Center in the case it had filed two years earlier against the city of San Antonio, and won.

In cities like San Antonio, Giuliani's jihad made political hay. During the same media season in which San Antonio native Kenneth Starr was pillorying Bill Clinton for his affair with Monica Lewinsky, Giuliani was appearing on *Meet the Press*, *This Week*, and *Fox News Sunday*, attacking Hillary's support of what he termed obscene and blasphemous museumology: "She agrees with using public funds to bash the Catholic religion," the mayor said. It was probably no coincidence that, to raise money for his Senate run, he had employed right-wing, direct-mail guru Richard Viguerie, who specialized in creating appeals tailored to religious zealots. A lawyer for the New York City chapter of the ACLU came across a Giuliani solicitation letter to Minnesota Republicans boasting of his desire to close the Brooklyn Museum. He also came out for prayer and the posting of the Ten Commandments in public schools.

Yet Giuliani's crusade got weak support locally. A poll conducted by *New York 1* and the *Daily News* found that residents backed the museum by two to one. Even Catholics in the city gave the mayor short shrift, by 48 to 42 percent. As Andrew Kirtzman wrote in his biography of the mayor, *Rudy Giuliani: Emperor of the City*, it was as though he was running for office against his own city.

And this time it wasn't just the poor or the outspoken who felt turned off.

Attorney John Wirenius, a native New Yorker, is a constitutional scholar who wrote a well-received and respected work of scholarship, *First Amendment Principles: Verbal Acts and Freedom of Speech*. He was in his early thirties in late 1997 when he began working as a lawyer for the city. He started in the general litigation division, specializing in the First Amendment.

"For awhile it was a great fit," he remembers. "I published the first edition of my book. And I was doing run-of-the-mill cases. Most were frivolous, lacking a real free speech claim." By the time the claims got serious, Wirenius was out of general litigation, working in another of the city's legal units, one that had nothing to do with the challenges brought against the city on First Amendment grounds.

The Brooklyn Museum blowup led to him being drafted as an advisor to city lawyers building the case for Giuliani's contention that the dung-adorned "Holy Virgin Mary" constituted libel against Catholics. The mayor's argument represented the very kind of direct affront to freedom of expression that Wirenius had denounced in his book. While acknowledging that much expression can be offensive, demeaning, and even deeply hurtful to groups such as women, Jews, and blacks, he'd written that the insult and pain must be borne because the First Amendment is too vital to be trifled with.

The experience of serving as a legal advisor for the city in the museum battle "split me in two," he says. "On the one hand, here I am working on one of the highest-profile cases of my career, and the natural desire of a lawyer to win was completely at war with the fact that as a First Amendment advocate and scholar, I knew we had to be smacked down, hard. And here I am, coming up with wild arguments that I had made fun of."

One of those arguments was inspired by the mayor's denunciation of Sensation as an attack on Catholics. In his book, Wirenius discusses *Beauharnais v. Illinois*, an obscure, 1950s-era case that began when a white racist was prosecuted for handing out leaflets in Chicago that heaped vitriol on blacks. Defendant Beauharnais exhausted his appeals, but even an unsympathetic U.S. Supreme Court ruled that his leaflets constituted "group libel" against an entire race. Wirenius felt the ruling had long ago been discredited and he ridiculed modern-day attempts to revive it as "ominous." Even so, to buttress Giuliani's claim that Sensation defamed an entire religious community, Wirenius found himself personally digging up *Beauharnais v. Illinois.*

Wirenius's wife, an artist who had posed with scores of others in the mid-1990s for a Spencer Tunick nude shot in Times Square, was appalled by what her husband was doing. His participation in the museum case, Wirenius remembers, "added a fair amount of mockery" to their relationship. Luckily, his colleagues decided to use other arguments instead of the one about group libel that Wirenius came up with.

Wirenius felt a pang of disappointment that morally horrified him. He started brooding during his daily commute to work. "Before the First Amendment free fall, I would walk from Church Street over the Brooklyn Bridge and look at the city before and behind me, and think, "I'm doing something good here. I thought of it as my city. The Brooklyn Museum burned that out of me."

Disgusted, Wirenius quit his job and went to work for the legal department at New York State United Teachers. He says that some of his colleagues quit as well.

The U.S. Court of Appeals for the Second District was also disgusted—and disturbed that it had, in effect, turned into a kind of shadow agency of City Hall in order to neutralize the Giuliani administration's endless assaults on free speech. In a majority opinion supporting Spencer Tunick's right to photograph nudes outdoors, published in early 2000, Circuit Judge Guido Calabresi noted that the Second District had handled eighteen cases in which it enjoined the city from carrying out policies or found them flat out unconstitutional. Such policies included prohibiting cops in a Latino police officers association from marching in uniform and with their group's banner in parades; making city employees get permission before speaking to the media; and limiting press conferences in front of City Hall to twenty-five people. "As a result of this relentless onslaught of First Amendment litigation," Calabresi continued, "the federal courts have, to a considerable extent, been drafted into the role of local licensors for the City of New York."

Few among the public studied Calabresi's ruling, but many read some boosterish news published in the same year as the circuit court's Tunick decision. Back in the mid-1990s, New York had been the nation's fifth most popular destination for American tourists. By 2000, the city had overtaken Las Vegas for number two, second only to Orlando, with its Disney World. "We're challenging Mickey Mouse," crowed Giuliani at a celebratory press conference.

San Antonio, meanwhile, proudly came in tenth on the list.

* * *

Six months after September 11, 2001, Giuliani visited San Antonio to attend the annual convention of the Yellow Pages Publishers Association. The group had just established a "Business Leader of the Year" award, and Giuliani would be the first person to receive it, one of scores of awards he garnered after the terror attack. The telephone-book people praised the former mayor not so much for his stewardship on 9/11, as for actions such as slashing the welfare rolls and, in general, creating "one of the greatest successes in business history: helping make New York the best known example of the resurgence of urban America."

A few months before the Yellow Pages convention—weeks after 9/11, in fact—the City of San Antonio had settled with Esperanza Center, agreeing to pay the group over a half million dollars after a court ruled that yanking its funding had been a First Amendment violation. There is no documentation in the San Antonio media that Giuliani went anywhere near the modest, heavily Hispanic neighborhood where Esperanza Center is located. Nor did he make any statements about the case that so closely resembled New York City's attempted assault on the Brooklyn Museum.

The press did note that Giuliani relaxed in San Antonio by playing a round of golf near the pretty neighborhood where cops ticketed teens for smoking on their lawns. Then he and girlfriend Judith Nathan dropped by a trendy restaurant, where they shared shrimp and steak. After the meal, he was asked by the owner to sign some T-shirts. Giuliani was more than happy to oblige.

The shirts were described as sporting an "Americana" logo. The owner planned to hang them on the restaurant walls. That way, tourists could pay homage to the logo and the autograph—which, by now, were presumed to be one and the same.

First Person
Steve Powers

THE "ELEPHANT DUNG," *available in sticky clumps at $1 a toss, was artificial, and the mayor's visage a cartoonish mockup. But the irreverent humor of the Saturday afternoon "Doody Rudy" protest in Washington Square Park in December 1999 was apparently lost on Giuliani's City Hall.*

Steve Powers of Manhattan didn't organize the protest of the mayor's threat to close down the Brooklyn Museum of Art; that was someone else's idea. But Powers was happy to contribute the satirical centerpiece. The mayor, who was cranking up a run for senator at the time, had objected most vocally to a museum exhibition of contemporary artist Chris Ofili's interpretation, The Holy Virgin Mary, *calling it anti-Catholic.*

Powers, a "graffiti artist," returned to his Greenwich Village apartment shortly before the rally to find five police officers conducting a raid and confiscating eight garbage bags filled with his art supplies, computer disks, and other property. eSPO, as his graffiti tag read, was taken downtown in handcuffs on a weapons possession charge after brass knuckles were found hanging on his kitchen wall—an ornament he once used as a design element for a hip hop magazine spread, he said. He was jailed five hours and released. The charges were subsequently dismissed.

"It was pretty ridiculous. I have to admit, I felt some kind of relief after this three-hour search—all my years of paranoia about being watched by the authorities was born out before my very eyes.

The whole situation just stunk. This is Giuliani. This is the way he operates. He made the call. I had just that day been on a radio talk show for five minutes promoting my book, *The Art of Getting Over*, a history of graffiti writers in New York and Philadelphia, and mentioned the schedule for the protest event at the very end of the broadcast.

The funny thing was, there were a lot worse graffiti writers out there. The type of graffiti I was writing involved painting over rolled down, rusted storefront gates, painting them silver and adding a few black lines to make it say eSPO.

That was about 90 percent of my output, far from the trains, highway signs, and the things that typically aggravate the populace. I was taking a very clean approach to what I was doing. I wasn't being nihilistic, and it wasn't a youthful stream of rebellion. It came from an artistic place in me, and I was in the last throes of it, transitioning into more of a fine-art career which I now have.

Well, the protest event. It would have drawn maybe fifty people. With my arrest, and the publicity, it gained a lot of momentum and poignancy. And it sent the message that this mayor is going to send his police force out to shut down dissenting voices—not even major ones, just someone doing an editorial cartoon in the middle of Washington Square Park. I would say that three hundred people showed up, plus, like, fifty cops.

When they asked the police commissioner, Howard Safir, about it, he told the press, oh, that guy, he's a criminal, he was in possession of a weapon, and we did the right thing. His comments were broadcast all over the television. I was scared because this guy was taking a personal interest in me. At the same time, there's a certain amount of notoriety that every graffiti writer wants. It was kind of backhanded praise, an elegant way for me to end this stage in my art.

I always disliked Giuliani. He gave me reason at the time to loathe him. When 9/11 came, I felt I can't hate this guy. But I would advise people to examine his record from September 10, 2001, on back. At the end of the day, he'll find a way to screw things up again. He's the victim of his own temper and temperament, especially when he has a real taste of the power. Once he treats America like he treated New York and really gets out of hand with it, forget about it."

Enforcement
Hugh Pearson

FOR ANYONE WHO wants to examine why African Americans despised Rudolph Giuliani, the March 16, 2000, police killing of Patrick Dorismond on the former mayor's watch about sums it up.

At about 12:30 a.m., Dorismond, a Haitian American security guard, and a fellow employee were celebrating the end of their shifts with a few beers at Wakamba Cocktail Lounge on Thirty-seventh Street and Eighth Avenue in Manhattan.

They decided to head for home and left the bar to hail a taxi. As they waited for a cab to stop, Dorismond was accosted by a Caucasian man who wanted to buy some marijuana.

I can imagine the scene myself. I personally have also encountered such Caucasians, who felt that, because of my brown skin and casual attire, I must have had drugs to sell or at least knew someone who did.

Before the inquisitive male stranger approached Dorismond outside the bar, Dorismond had faced similar dicey situations. He had been arrested thrice before, resulting in convictions for offenses no more serious or concrete than disorderly conduct. Dorismond became quite angry that the Caucasian thought he was a dealer.

Perhaps the discovery that the individual in question was a plain-clothes police officer only further enraged Dorismond, reminding him of his previous hassles with the police. A scuffle ensued, a backup officer fired a shot at Dorismond, and soon Patrick Dorismond was crumpled up on the pavement, dead at twenty-six.

As anyone who knows what life is like in New York City can attest, it is all too easy for encounters on the city's streets to escalate into heated arguments, especially when you add race to the brew, and you happen to be, like me, an African American male. It happens to be very easy for any African American male to unfairly acquire an arrest and conviction record. And it is very easy for African American males to become involved in arguments that can turn heated on the streets.

Because, even though the killing of Dorismond, a security guard by profession, spawned a huge furor from a city still disquieted if not outraged by the killing one year earlier of a weaponless West African named Amadou Diallo, shot by Caucasian plainclothes officers from the cowboy-like Street Crimes Unit whose motto was "We own the night." Giuliani defended the two police officers involved in Dorismond's death.

Memorably—infamously—Giuliani flagged, Joe McCarthy–style, the late Dorismond's sealed arrest record. It consisted of those three convictions for the horrendous crime of disorderly conduct—from which Giuliani concluded that Dorismond had been no altar boy. In fact, Dorismond had served as an altar boy when he was growing up, his grieving family noted.

Here was Rudy once again in knee-jerk mode, ratcheting up police-community tensions and racial heat. He discredited the victim's reputation by releasing Dorismond's private, sealed-by-the-court juvenile record. If he thought his fevered antics would help him court conservative white voters across the state in his U.S. Senate race that year, he was wrong. Giuliani backed out of that race and some observers regarded his handling of this case as a crystallization of his worst tendencies.

The racial atmosphere in the city became tense, to say the least. But Giuliani said he would not shift gears and that doing so would be a concession to criminals. He'd professed to be race-blind, anyway. So the hard-line police department proceeded on autopilot, although public-safety conditions across the city had eased dramatically compared to the years of soaring gun violence. Not long after the Dorismond tragedy, police officers chased a suspected marijuana dealer through a crowded schoolyard in the largely African American Bedford-Stuyvesant section of Brooklyn. What resulted was a stampede in which three children were hurt as they watched or tried to get out of the way while cops drew their side arms and arrested the suspect. It was part of the same general sweep that had resulted in Dorismond's killing, Operation Condor, designed to get marijuana dealers and buyers off the streets.

* * *

Rudolph Giuliani was the type of politician who smeared and divided, who didn't care about the wreckage he caused in the lives of thousands of African Americans and, to a lesser extent, Hispanic New Yorkers, in his much-applauded efforts to "take back the streets of New York City from the criminals."

He was also the type who didn't care when he was wrapping his 1993 opponent, David Dinkins, the only African American mayor in the city's history, with the fallacious charge of running a city into near chaos. Giuliani, like his foil the Reverend Al Sharpton, had no problem fanning the flames of racial suspicion and hate when he thought it would further his career. He shamelessly used the New York City police department, the city's front line troops in his war on crime, to realize his political aspirations.

In my opinion, there are few redeeming qualities to the NYPD. Of course there are many exceptions among the nearly forty thousand officers on the force, but the typical officer treats the typical African American male as if he is guilty of something until proven innocent. And just to prove how racist to its core the police department happens to be, during the Dinkins administration hundreds of officers staged a 1993 rally in front of City Hall, in which officers deployed racial epithets against Mayor Dinkins—their pickets referred to him as a washroom attendant—with candidate Giuliani on hand to egg them on through a bullhorn. As a result of the belief that Dinkins hadn't allowed the police to conduct business as usual in African American and Latino communities, police officers throughout the city and their bellicose labor leaders overwhelmingly supported the election of Giuliani as mayor that year.

Giuliani turned around as mayor and gave them what they wanted, albeit no raises in light of severe budgetary constraints in his first term. And he used the excuse of fast-declining crime as a shield for allowing officers to return to the days when they could relax and once more treat "unsavory elements" as "gorillas in the mist." If anything went fatally astray, cops could count on their apologist in City Hall to give them the benefit of the doubt.

All of this is not to say that the crime reduction that took place on Giuliani's watch was anything but impressive. When Giuliani took office there were more than two thousand homicides per year in New York City, mainly in poor neighborhoods. By the time Giuliani left office at the end of 2001, the city's murder rate had fallen by 70 percent, reaching its lowest level since 1964. Overall, violent crime rates went down by half. This change, in keeping with or exceeding the national trend, benefited blacks as well as Caucasians.

Yet some conservative commentators who have praised Giuliani's crime-fighting successes failed to credit David Dinkins for the increase in police recruits that he set in motion while in office. Commentators have also failed to acknowledge that the Safe Streets strategy launched by Dinkins and his police commissioner, Ray Kelly, was already having an impact when Giuliani's first term began; that civic leaders, and particularly churches, had played a significant role in curbing violence in their neighborhoods; and that young people themselves were turning away from a life of drugs and guns, which had crippled and nearly wiped out their communities in the 1980s.

New York City's crime rate had climbed sky-high before Dinkins took office, when Abe Beame and Ed Koch were in charge. It was under Beame, not Dinkins, that President Gerald Ford had refused to bail out the city from the devastating consequences of its fiscal irresponsibility. The city, with its graffiti-covered subways, became synonymous with urban blight in the 1970s and 1980s, causing Hollywood to create Charles Bronson–type cinematic scenarios in which vigilante justice was meted out, usually against African Americans or Hispanics.

* * *

David Dinkins certainly wasn't the perfect mayor. Being the career government employee that he was—part of the city's Harlem political machine, a man who only reluctantly agreed to run for mayor in 1989—he was hardly the best candidate African American New York City could have put forward. But neither did he deserve the unremittingly bad rap his critics, led by Giuliani, gave him—a rap that, given Giuliani's political uses for polarization politics, was related to the color of his skin.

Furthermore, despite all the pride some observers feel in the "return of New York City," such a renaissance was certainly achievable without incidents such as the Diallo and Dorismond killings.

The unfortunate truth is that the crime reductions realized under Giuliani were achieved on the backs of too many innocent African American New Yorkers. Thousands of African Americans were arrested on usually contrived misdemeanor charges, such as riding a bicycle without a bell on the handlebars or hanging around in a park. The purpose was to check them for weapons or outstanding warrants. They usually were jailed overnight before ever seeing a judge. Almost invariably, judges tossed out the alleged offense as a ridiculous waste of a backlogged court's time.

That such offensive treatment of African Americans was par for the course under Giuliani was a finding confirmed by the task force appointed by the mayor himself in the uproar that followed the 1997 torture and sodomizing of Abner Louima, a Haitian-American, by cops in a Brooklyn stationhouse bathroom—the same task force whose findings the mayor went on to impugn.

Four years later, the tragic deaths of twenty-three police officers on 9/11 created a welter of sympathy for the police. Many citizens forgot that the modus operandi used by the city's police force has been tantamount to catching a thousand fish to net one shark. In the same way, lowering the threshold of evidence needed to separate children from the homes of poor families in which neglect or abuse was alleged was effective during the Giuliani years. However, too often, parents who were innocent of neglect and abuse saw their children taken away, and many others lived in continuous fear of it happening to their families.

One of the sad and troubling "lessons" of the Giuliani years is that when New Yorkers, especially police, now think of reducing crime, it's still a euphemism for "controlling the coons and spics," as in those 1970s vigilante-justice movies. Too few people in politics or the criminal justice system want to engage in the hard work and public expense of ensuring that innocent African Americans and Hispanics are differentiated from criminals and protected from crime the way many Caucasians are.

Giuliani allowed the NYPD to run roughshod over the city's non-Caucasian communities to achieve the statistical results he needed to further his career. What a price the city paid for its comeback. But then, among those who count in the eyes of the city's powers-that-be, who really gives a damn? In no small part thanks to Giuliani, the prevailing attitude appears to be "One couldn't have made the good omelet called the New York City Renaissance without breaking a lot of African American and Hispanic eggs."

First Person
Margarita Rosario

MARGARITA ROSARIO'S SON, Anthony, *was fatally shot at the age of eighteen after showing up at an apartment in the Morris Heights section of the Bronx with his cousin, twenty-one-year-old Hilton Vega, on January 12, 1995.*

They were killed by detectives who fired twenty-two shots, also wounding a third young man. The detectives had served as bodyguards in Rudolph Giuliani's unsuccessful 1989 mayoral race. They maintained that they staked out the apartment on a tip that a robbery was about to take place. They felt in imminent danger of being shot and contended Anthony and Hilton did not obey orders to drop to the floor.

Freddie Bonilla, who was shot in the leg, maintained that Hilton and Anthony had gone to the apartment that night to collect a debt owed to Hilton's girlfriend. Hilton had invited Anthony to come along.

An autopsy found that Anthony and his cousin were lying face down when they were shot. A Bronx grand jury did not indict the detectives. However, the Civilian Complaint Review Board found the police used unnecessary and excessive force.

Rosario, who contends that Bonilla and another witness to the shooting were never brought before the grand jury, founded Mothers Against Police Brutality and became a familiar presence at protest rallies. On a Friday morning in July 1999, she called Giuliani's weekly radio show and got through. After offering up a few pleasantries, she began to challenge the mayor's past portrayals of the shooting, trying to suggest that they were inaccurate. She did not get very far. Giuliani repeatedly cut her off, labeling her son a "criminal who wanted to kill other people."

"He said to me, 'You have to look at your background, the church you went to, the school, the way you raised your son.' He got me nervous. I had trouble thinking clearly. He sounded almost like a father defending his two sons in the way he blasted at me, saying that I raised my child in a horrible manner, and the cops were doing their jobs against two criminals. My son did not have a criminal record. He had never been in jail.

I knew Giuliani was a bully. I was expecting somewhat of an attitude from him. But I was also hoping, I guess, for a little bit of consideration. It didn't happen. His comments hurt. They hurt a lot. It was right around the time of my son's birthday. I got very emotional at that time.

What you want? You want safer streets, then you gotta pay a price! That was the mayor's attitude. But why should I pay a price in the blood of my child? No I tell you, there was an epidemic of police brutality going on. The mothers who lost their children under extremely questionable circumstances had to bring attention to it, and in many, many different ways, we did.

I see now that Rudy Giuliani has made himself the hero of 9/11, it's amazing. But the heroes were the police officers and the firemen and the paramedics, the people who went in to help. Those were the heroes. Rudy did absolutely nothing to prevent 9/11 or help the people trapped in the towers.

My own feeling is Giuliani has to be totally investigated, from the bottom of his soles to his hair, because there's more to this man than we see on the surface. Could you imagine if he became president some day? The way he was, the way he did things that he did, and no one could question him. He has a dictator type of personality."

Shelter
Glenn Thrush

IN THE SPRING of 1998, the Reverend Calvin Butts, a powerful Harlem preacher and a Democrat with few compunctions about endorsing Republicans like George Pataki, was so outraged at Rudy Giuliani's response to the shooting of unarmed African immigrant Amadou Diallo, he told a TV reporter the mayor was a "racist."

During his three decades in public life, no insult has aroused Giuliani's ire quite so much as being called a bigot. Enraged by Butts's comments, Giuliani took swift action: he ordered his sole African American deputy mayor, Rudy Washington, to block the renovation of the Astor Row Homes on West 130th Street and called a halt to the planned construction of eighty units of low-income housing in another part of Harlem. Both projects were dear to the reverend's heart and, not coincidentally, developed by the Abyssinian Development Corporation, the housing arm of his church.

The irony that a vengeful white mayor would scuttle much-needed housing for working-class African Americans just to prove he wasn't a racist was apparently lost on a politician who was, in the best of times, irony challenged.

It took weeks of frantic negotiations and make-nice gestures by Butts to repair the relationship, but that didn't stop the mayor from handing off the projects to other developers. By 1999, the two men were on speaking terms, and both projects sailed ahead.

The Butts episode was just one in a series of mayoral actions that illustrated the priority, ranging from low to lower, that the Giuliani administration placed on housing development. Housing, particularly in the city's poorest neighborhoods, was simply off the map at City Hall, and individual projects were never beyond being used as pawns on Giuliani's political and personal chessboard.

That said, there's no doubt that life improved greatly in New York's lower-income neighborhoods during Giuliani's reign. The explanation, like almost everything else that happened from 1994 through 2001 in New York, can be attributed to Giuliani's obsession with cleaning up crime.

Drug dealing—like day care—is a business best conducted close to home, so when Giuliani helped clean up neighborhoods of criminals, he was also increasing the value of the real estate that dealers had long devalued. Crime-fighting turned out to be a development strategy.

The ripple effect of safer streets was galvanizing. Less fear meant more development, much of it in the form of new one- and two-family houses built in neighborhoods like East New York, Brooklyn, that had been free-fire zones as recently as the early 1990s. It also meant the revival of a once-endangered species in the inner-city: middle-class African American homeowners.

A longtime housing organizer in East New York—Mike Gecan of the Metro Industrial Areas Foundation—described the scene in an article he wrote in early 2004, a decade after the Brooklyn neighborhood had been overrun by gun-toting drug dealers. "A new homeowner, all five feet and one inch of her, takes a walk in the evening with her lady friend through streets that used to be too dangerous for DEA agents wearing bulletproof vests," Gecan wrote in the *Village Voice*.

Still, for most of the decade, Giuliani and his team devoted little attention to actual housing development, a crucial mistake that helped worsen an already severe shortage of reasonably affordable housing. Housing statistics are hard to massage or manipulate. And Giuliani's housing record, by the numbers, points to a mayoralty of squandered opportunities, diminished expectations, and a lack of foresight.

During the middle and late 1990s, almost no new rental buildings were put up in working class neighborhoods, although immigrants were pouring into the city at a record clip. In these years, New York City's population grew by 456,000, but only 82,000 new housing units were produced.

The city, which by 1998 was swimming in budget surpluses nearing $2.5 billion, could have filled the breach by helping to finance an even greater number of apartment renovations or new construction. Instead, the opposite happened. As federal subsidies dried up in the Republican-controlled U.S. House of Representatives, Giuliani systematically gutted the city's own financial commitments, which had peaked in the 1980s under then-mayor Ed Koch.

In last fiscal year of Koch's tenure, the city shelled out $737.2 million in capital payments for housing. When combined with federal aid, the total spent climbed to more than $1.1 billion per year, after being adjusted for inflation.

The city's contribution was slowed by the recession of the early 1990s, when David Dinkins was mayor for one term, but it was Giuliani who turned off the taps. By 1996, the middle of Giuliani's first four years in office, the city was spending less than a third of its 1989 capital budget on housing—about $200 million. The total would trail off to $140 million in 1998, according to an analysis by local housing advocate Joe Weisbrod, who describes Giuliani's housing policy as "massive, systematic disinvestment."

"The trouble," a Giuliani-era housing official aide told me in 1997, "is that nobody at the whole agency really gives a shit about the issue of housing anymore."

* * *

The Giuliani administration's policies wouldn't have been as damaging if private market rents weren't at the same time exceeding the reach of the working poor. True, the explosion of real estate prices created a generation of brownstone millionaires in Brooklyn neighborhoods like Park Slope and Fort Greene. But they also helped to raise real estate values—and rents—in previously dirt-cheap havens like Highbridge in the Bronx.

In part, the pattern of rent increases was a byproduct of the Koch-era rehabilitation of about two hundred thousand units of dilapidated buildings, primarily in the Bronx and Brooklyn, an investment that reversed a decades-long history of abandonment and blight that led to the arson fires that swept through the Bronx—made famous by a sweeping camera shot of the smoldering borough during the 1977 World Series. They were also a byproduct of Giuliani's achievements in reducing crime in all neighborhoods.

As a measure of the city's economic health, the climbing cost of housing was a good thing. But for poor people struggling in low-wage jobs, it simply meant having to shell out more rent than they could afford. "If you want to move into a nice place, you are going to have to pay a lot," one Highbridge resident told me in 1997 after her landlord jacked her monthly rent from $572 to $700. "If the building is new and clean, people don't really mind. But people are paying $700 a month for rat holes."

It would only get worse. By the end of the 1990s, more than 500,000 city families—one in four—were paying more than half of their income for rent, far more than the third of gross earnings that the federal government considers affordable. Indeed, between 1993 and 1996, the city lost 20 percent of its apartments renting for under $500 a month, a total of 110,000 units for working families.

*   *   *

It's difficult to know whether the record rates of homelessness in the city following Giuliani's departure from City Hall resulted from his policy of choking off the city's investments in affordable housing. But there's evidence his decisions played at least some role.

What's undeniable is that homelessness, which initially afflicted de-institutionalized mentally ill adults in the 1980s, evolved into a massive family homelessness crisis for the city during Giuliani's tenure. For the roots of family homelessness are found in a lack of cheap, habitable housing—exactly the supply that dwindled in the five boroughs on Giuliani's watch.

Responsibility for addressing the problem has fallen to Giuliani's successor, Michael Bloomberg. During Giuliani's first full year in office, there were 24,000 homeless people in city shelters. In Bloomberg's first full year as mayor, the number spiked to a record-shattering 35,000, a 46 percent increase.

But the most alarming statistic by far was the explosion in the number of children in city homeless shelters. Their presence increased to record levels as families were drawn to the shelter system—the most convenient entry point for eventually obtaining a subsidized apartment. In 1995 there were 9,927 children in the shelter system on any given night. By 2002, that number had increased by 50 percent to a staggering 14,952.

In a clear break with Giuliani, Mayor Bloomberg embarked on a plan to renovate 65,000 units of affordable housing in the city. He also emphasized that finding permanent apartments for homeless families is the main objective of his housing agenda.

* * *

No aspect of this crisis would have been apparent from listening to Giuliani talk about his mayoral legacy in recent years. In numerous pronouncements, he has emphasized one aspect of his housing record: his successful drive to divest the city of its deteriorating stock of inner-city apartment buildings seized from slumlords in the 1970s and 1980s for their failure to pay delinquent real estate taxes.

When he took office, the city's ownership of this infamous "In Rem" stock was hovering at around 31,000 apartments. By the time he left City Hall, that number had shriveled to about 5,700, an 80 percent reduction.

The policy of selling off the buildings to private developers had begun in previous administrations. But the increases in property values across the city, coupled with a spate of Clinton-era tax breaks, gave investors an incentive to rehabilitate buildings in low-income neighborhoods.

Giuliani didn't pioneer the process, but he injected it with new vigor, pushing for the transfer of buildings as fast as private landlords and community-development organizations could structure complex transactions to patch up the properties.

New York City had first begun harvesting this pipeline of dilapidated buildings during the 1980s. Mayor Koch, faced with the first waves of homelessness, began his unparalleled, ten-year investment of $5 billion to rehabilitate abandoned housing.

While usually quick to accept plaudits, Koch has uncharacteristically played down his housing record, though many observers have cited it as his most lasting accomplishment. Giuliani suffered from no similar attack of modesty.

In the mid-1990s, with rents rising and the city's investment in affordable housing shriveled, Giuliani seized on the idea of getting rid of the remaining stock of foreclosed buildings as an opportunity for publicity. The strategy was subtle and savvy. Other administrations had measured their housing success in concrete terms, such as the number of poor families successfully placed in affordable apartments. But that approach—later embraced by Mayor Bloomberg—implicitly recognizes that there is a housing crisis. That admission might well have put the focus on Giuliani's cuts to the city's housing budget. So Giuliani didn't talk much about housing, but when he did he almost always emphasized the "In Rem" policy, to the exclusion of far less flattering statistics. During his carefully stage-managed annual management reports, the sell-off of city properties was plotted on a huge cliff-like graph, with thousands of unwanted apartments tumbling into oblivion.

The truer story was being told on the walls of the city's Department of Housing Preservation and Development—papered with announcements for employees' retirement parties.

Once regarded as the best public development agency in the nation, the department was ground down by attrition, forced transfers, and a succession of frustrated commissioners in the Giuliani years.

The housing department suffered the defection of its institutional knowledge and experience, as its development chief, its planning and sales director, and the head of its emergency repair program all left. Gone too were nearly one hundred of the mid-level technocrats who had accumulated years of housing expertise necessary to make the "In Rem" strategy work.

In 1998, after the departure of two housing commissioners in only three years, Giuliani tapped Richard Roberts, a thirty-four-year-old hospital public relations officer who knew little about housing but a lot about networking. His father-in-law was Vernon Jordan, one of President Clinton's closest friends.

* * *

It was shortly after Roberts took over the department that the Giuliani administration took on another powerful black clergyman with an ambitious housing project before the city.

The Reverend Johnnie Ray Youngblood had a huge proposal that required Giuliani's approval—a five-hundred-apartment development in a swampy stretch of East New York in Brooklyn that the mayor had personally endorsed from Youngblood's own pulpit in 1995. The support disappeared when Youngblood, founder of the Nehemiah Project, which had erected thousands of new apartments, staked claim to a cluster of Harlem baseball fields against City Hall's wishes.

To Youngblood's amazement, Roberts responded by revoking $5 million that the city had slated for needed infrastructure improvements for the Spring Creek project. Giuliani, in turn, likened the preacher's housing plan to a sacred cow.

"Sacred cows make the best hamburger meat," the mayor declared.

In the end, it was Roberts who went through the grinder. In 2002 he resigned another city post after he was caught pawning off a $600 New Orleans strip club bill on a city credit card. Two years later, he pleaded guilty to lying to federal investigators who were investigating his misuse of a $38,000 city-owned SUV.

At this writing, Youngblood was still toiling to get his Spring Creek project built.

Integrity

Dan Janison

*"The choice of a prince's ministers is a matter of no little
importance; they are either good or not according to the prudence of
the prince. The first impression one gets of a ruler and of his brains
is from seeing the men that he has about him."*
—Niccolo Machiavelli, 1513

ON MARCH 17, 2003, the U.S. attorney for the Southern District
of New York announced a criminal indictment charging Russell A.
Harding, former president of the New York City Housing
Development Corporation, with participation in a scheme to
defraud his agency of hundreds of thousands of dollars and with
receiving and possessing child pornography.

Harding's father Ray, the canny and sophisticated boss of the
Liberal Party of New York, was the closest of political advisers to
Rudolph Giuliani. Ray Harding's older son Robert served as one of
Giuliani's four deputy mayors. When Russell Harding was tapped
for this executive housing post in 1998, some City Hall reporters
questioned the fact that he had neither relevant experience nor even
a college degree. Giuliani publicly dismissed those concerns.

Early in 2002, shortly after the mayoralty changed, Russell
Harding left the agency. By then he had "illegally used HDC funds
for his own personal gain and for the personal benefit of friends and

associates," said U.S. Attorney James B. Comey. Harding "sought to evade detection by falsely characterizing improper personal expenses as legitimate business expenses, and concealed and destroyed evidence that would have revealed these illegal activities," said a joint statement from the leading accusers—Comey and the city Department of Investigation, newly headed by Rose Gill Hearn, an appointee of Giuliani's successor as mayor, Michael Bloomberg.

On this day the authorities employed the kind of indignant rhetoric Giuliani used on similar occasions in the 1980s when he was U.S. attorney. Comey stated that Russell Harding sought to "create his own version of *Lifestyles of the Rich and Famous*" with money from HDC, which the government created to finance the building and repair of affordable housing. "The embezzlement with which he is charged," said Comey, "ran the gamut from obtaining a $38,000 vehicle for personal use of a friend, to personal trips and the purchase of books and videos which he then attempted to cover up. He was generous to a fault. Except the fault was that the money was the public's, which is a federal crime." On March 15, 2005, Harding pleaded guilty in the case, facing fifty-one to sixty-three months in prison.

The Harding conviction belonged to a cluster of cases that showed Giuliani's City Hall to have been in some measure vulnerable to the kind of corruption he had once made his reputation inveighing against. Because these prosecutions played out after Giuliani left office, however, their revelations were less than newsworthy. Fortunately for the ex-mayor's image, these prosecutions were treated in most news media as isolated footnotes or curiosities. By then the two-term Republican had become "America's Mayor" to the millions of television viewers impressed with his public conduct in the wake of the September 11, 2001, attack.

But this handful of corruption cases forms a kind of eclipsed epilogue to the Giuliani years. Examined in the absence of media spin and information control, which any incumbent mayor gets to exercise, these cases reveal the deficiencies of what was, in the end, an ordinary city government doing business in the traditional manner of local politics.

* * *

On December 31, 2001, Giuliani and his top aides strode out the door of City Hall to the sentimental skirl of ceremonial bagpipes. Two months later, the U.S. attorney's office announced the arrest of eighteen current or former city tax assessors. For more than thirty years, it was charged, the eighteen veteran employees had accepted more than $10 million in bribes to alter the assessed values of more than five hundred properties. Over Giuliani's final term, prosecutors charged, the city lost $40 million a year in tax revenues to the scam.

To be sure, the city Finance Department and internal city investigators participated and cooperated in the probe of the tax assessors. Once the case was announced, though, ex-Giuliani officials claimed the feds' loss-of-revenue evaluation was overstated. The question spurred by the case would never be resolved. The case was aborted when a central figure in the scandal, the octogenarian defendant Albert Schussler, passed away. Several of those indicted took plea deals. Left behind was an errant part of the city's sprawling bureaucracy that had gone unreformed despite Giuliani's image as a stern overseer of government agencies.

In the city's Buildings Department, bribery cases involving elevator inspectors, building inspectors, and borough supervisors cropped up continually as they had under the Democratic administrations that preceded Giuliani. Other messes, of course, never rose to the level of prosecution but did raise concerns among governmental monitors and civic activists independent of the mayor's office. One controversy arose over the dubious purchase and use of highly flammable stairwell paint in city Housing Authority projects. Another involved the Human Resources Administration, where a dispute with the comptroller's office over the propriety of multi-million-dollar welfare-to-work processing contracts turned out to involve a social services company headed by Giuliani's former welfare adviser.

A more fertile spawning ground for prosecution proved to be the middle-to-upper ranks of the Correction Department. The scandals there began more than two years before the agency's former commissioner, Bernard Kerik, a Giuliani associate, withdrew as President George W. Bush's designee for U.S. homeland security secretary in late 2004 amid questions about his personal and business lives. When Giuliani left City Hall and Bloomberg settled in, the department was still headed by a member of what had been Kerik's inner circle, a commissioner who resigned under a cloud eleven months into the new administration.

It is easy to see why so many of the problems at the Correction Department had eluded scrutiny during the Giuliani years. In tandem with nationwide reductions in crime, jails became less crowded and less violent during Giuliani's tenure than they had been in a generation—like the crime decline, part of a national trend. Measures against officer-on-inmate abuse were ordered by the courts, efforts were launched to weed out gang activity, and more systematic searches made weapons less plentiful.

Up the management ranks in the 1990s came a man named Anthony Serra. This high-ranking jails chief, it turned out, was with his commissioner's blessing collecting hundreds of thousands of dollars on the side to provide security for the state Republican Party. Serra was at the same time organizing "volunteers" from among his subordinates to help the re-election efforts of Republican Governor George Pataki. It would later be charged by the Bronx district attorney's office that Serra was illegally running a Republican campaign operation from his office at Rikers Island and getting correction officers to spend their workdays renovating his home in Rockland County, New York. Ultimately Serra would plead guilty to state felony and misdemeanor counts, as well as federal tax-evasion charges. In a civil court, meanwhile, came allegations by deputy warden Lionel Lorquet, who claimed in a lawsuit that he was videotaped outside his house and punitively transferred for the political transgression of volunteering for Democratic mayoral candidate Mark Green in the 2001 race to succeed Giuliani. Lorquet swore that Serra told him, after Bloomberg beat Green that November, that Lorquet had "joined the wrong team and that if he had joined chief Serra's team he would have done better career-wise."

In January 2004, the Bloomberg administration agreed to pay Lorquet a $325,000 out-of-court settlement even as city lawyers announced that the jail system "acted appropriately and does not admit any fault." As this developed, Bloomberg aides also halted the correction officers union's practice of using city-paid "release time" to send its department delegates to work for selected candidates as they had in the past.

* * *

Other unfortunate cases came from places that fell formally outside the offices of government.

In November 2003, the U.S. attorney for the Eastern District, Roslynn Mauskopf, announced criminal charges against Steve Zakheim, the forty-nine-year-old president of one of the largest private ambulance companies in the city.

Zakheim was accused of funneling illegal campaign contributions totalling $32,500 to five federal political committees in 1998 and 1999. One of these was the Friends of Giuliani Exploratory Committee, set up in anticipation of the 2000 Senate campaign; another was a Giuliani entity called Solutions America. While Mauskopf said at the time that these campaigns were not culpable, the text of the indictment included something quite pointed. It said that in February 2000, following his contributions, Zakheim's company became the first for-profit company ever approved by the city for a contract allowing its ambulances to respond to 911 emergency calls.

"The lucrative contract," states count sixty-one of the Zakheim indictment, "was not subject to competitive bidding, but required approval from the mayor."

* * *

Troubles also arose from nonprofit entities created to raise and disburse off-budget funds under the direction of city officials. The most serious was the bizarre case of Frederick J. Patrick, who during the Giuliani administration had served as deputy corrections commissioner for programs, deputy coordinator for criminal justice services, and finally, as commissioner of the Department of Juvenile Justice. In these jobs, Patrick earned praise. But he ran into trouble as treasurer of the New York Correction Foundation Inc. and, apparently, had been made the sole signatory on its bank account. In July 2003, U.S.

Attorney David Kelley's office charged that Patrick, by then a deputy police commissioner under Bloomberg, had misappropriated foundation funds, mostly to pay for more than $110,000 worth of phone calls—of a "personal" nature, collected from inmates—between 1997 and 2001. Patrick pleaded guilty to two counts of mail fraud. On June 24, 2004, at age thirty-nine, Patrick was sentenced to serve a year and a day in federal prison.

During his mayoralty, Giuliani also asserted influence over quasi-public business improvement districts, in which the local merchants pay fees for extra sweeping, garbage pickup, and special lighting along shopping strips and in outdoor malls. These are non-government entities subject to city regulation through its business-services department. Lou Carbonetti, a childhood friend of Giuliani, came to run a business improvement district (BID) in Brooklyn. When he pleaded guilty to three counts of perjury involving a private contract in February 2004, it echoed an earlier mess. Nine years earlier this same mayoral friend was forced to resign as Giuliani's Community Affairs Unit director when it was revealed that he had failed to report more than $150,000 in debts, including unpaid taxes, on official disclosure forms. (Carbonetti's son, Anthony, is now an aide to Giuliani in the former mayor's private consulting business.)

The city does have a Department of Investigation (DOI) to battle internal municipal corruption and to refer criminal cases to prosecutors. Giuliani kept it on a tight leash. Prior to the mayor's departure from office, the New York City Housing Development Corporation told the *Village Voice* that documents related to Russell Harding's alleged misdeeds could not be found. But the publication received the material after Giuliani left and Bloomberg took office and put Hearn in charge of the DOI. She'd also taken up the Carbonetti case—after her predecessor was gone.

In his first term, Giuliani was asked why his DOI commissioner at the time, Howard Wilson, sat in on city strategy meetings and reported to the mayor and his cabinet on the progress of secret investigations of city employees. To be sure, the mayor's rationale for this new practice was sensible and persuasive enough. Ultimately, he said, he was the one elected to be responsible for the substance and tone of city government. But for Giuliani in this case, setting the tone meant controlling the message. Indeed, back in 1993, a differently configured, more independent DOI had publicly reported on irregularities in the way a city Transportation Department contractor was selected—just as Mayor David Dinkins was running for re-election. No such political awkwardness would be permitted by Dinkins's successor.

In a similar vein, Giuliani's ministers fiercely prevented outside agencies from infringing on the mayor's domain as those ministers defined it—even if these outsiders thought they had the idea of checks-and-balances on their side. During Giuliani's tenure, the oversight and reach of the city and state comptrollers, the public advocate, City Council committees, federal agencies, and state and federal courts would be challenged by city lawyers, with decidedly mixed success, involving issues as varied as welfare policy, police abuses, and economic development.

Even critics of Giuliani who are bent on romanticizing spirited New York street flavor and grieving its loss during the 1990s have cause to cheer up. As the record would later show, the prince and his ministers left behind no more and no less than their share of grit. Nearly three years after Giuliani left office, prosecutors were claiming more targets. With the Russell Harding case still unresolved, the former housing commissioner and hospitals board chairman Richard Roberts—another Giuliani appointee—pleaded guilty to lying to officials investigating the misuse of funds at the city's Housing Development Corporation during Harding's rule.

This was at the beginning of September 2004, during the Republican National Convention at Madison Square Garden. Specifically, Roberts pleaded guilty to a felony in Manhattan federal court. He admitted that after leaving government service, he drove a $38,000 sport utility vehicle purchased by HDC—the same SUV mentioned in Harding's indictment eighteen months earlier.

Message
Richard Steier

MOMENTS AFTER RUDOLPH Giuliani's former police, fire, and emergency management commissioners finished testifying May 18, 2004, before the federal panel examining the World Trade Center terror attack, reporters witnessed a familiar sight: a press photographer being manhandled by a bodyguard after getting too close.

Bernard Kerik, who was once the city's police commissioner; Tom Von Essen, the former fire commissioner; and Richard Sheier, the previous director of emergency management, had formed an impromptu huddle with other members of Giuliani's private consulting firm. They were discussing what they'd tell the media about the harsh and skeptical questions from members of the 9/11 commission about New York's poorly coordinated emergency response. The photographer had approached the trio in pursuit of a candid tableau in the courtyard of The New School University in Greenwich Village, and a beefy man in a suit had moved in and shoved him away.

"You know you're not supposed to do that!" the photographer shouted at the bodyguard. Then Sunny Mindel, the former mayoral press aide who was now communications director for Giuliani's private consulting firm, tried to restore order.

The scene was a blast from Giuliani's embattled mayoralty, and the moment didn't infuse most observers with a nostalgic glow. In fact it was characteristic of the Giuliani administration's determination—subtle when possible, heavy-handed when not—to bar access to anyone trying to determine independently whether reality matched the mayor's self-congratulatory rhetoric about his governance of the city.

The attempts to treat reporters, at best, like mushrooms—keeping them in the dark and feeding them plenty of manure—persisted right up to Giuliani's departure from office December 31, 2001. They were capped by a classic Giuliani bid for control of the flow of information concerning his record—and are well worth remembering since he apparently wants to run for higher office someday.

With only days to go before the end of his second and last term—and notably after he had tried to lengthen it beyond the statutory limit in the crisis atmosphere following 9/11—Giuliani quietly arranged to cut off all public access to his mayoral papers by researchers and reporters for years to come. If anyone was going to define his legacy, at least while the media and historians were still keenly interested, it was going to be him and his cadre of mayoral aides.

Much to the chagrin of historians, who would soon assemble on the City Hall steps to decry the unprecedented maneuver, Giuliani had his official papers removed from City Hall to a secure, windowless art warehouse in Queens.

Previous mayors had left behind their official papers in the municipal archives, where they were open to inspection. The controlling and secretive Giuliani would have none of that. One of his aides defended the stealth move amid the public uproar, saying the documents were carried out in preparation for the creation of a presidential-style library that would be called the Rudolph W. Giuliani Center for Urban Affairs.

In the end, however, Giuliani agreed to having all the papers—taxpayer-owned property, after all—shipped to the municipal archives a block from City Hall. But he would do it his way, gradually and selectively, leaving aside potentially embarrassing material.

Instead of a file on Peter Powers, the childhood friend and trusted deputy mayor with whom Giuliani had a falling-out over the ubiquitous influence of his first press secretary, Cristyne Lategano, the municipal archives received the papers of Powers's comparatively little-known assistant, Gordon Campbell. The file from

Campbell, who became homeless services commissioner after Powers left the administration, consisted of mundane items such as canned speeches delivered before audiences of civic leaders, real estate investors, and senior citizens.

Another Giuliani administration figure, Randy Mastro, was the deputy mayor who doled out patronage to labor leaders in return for union endorsements during Giuliani's 1997 re-election campaign, but the early archival deposits on labor issues included no papers on the sensitive topic; instead they were heavy with such benign documents as articles clipped from newspapers and union newsletters, and scintillating details of poll ratings.

It was clear that the choicest nuggets in the Giuliani file—can anyone find former deputy mayor John Dyson's leaked memo urging Giuliani to resist pressure to integrate the predominantly white and male top ranks of his administration?—were missing and probably would remain so until Giuliani has completed his anticipated run for state or national office, if they ever make it into the archives at all. The innocuous selections were enough to make one wonder whether the spicier items, more telling than the press releases and invitations, were never meant to leave the warehouse where Giuliani originally stored them.

One of the many things wrong with excessive secrecy is it allows serious troubles to thrive without exposure and breeds suspicion and distrust.

The most glaring example was the case of Russell Harding, a reflection of nepotism and cronyism that significantly compromised city government operations during the Giuliani years and was especially notable since Giuliani had campaigned for mayor as the antidote for decades of Democratic Party patronage and corruption.

That this one high-level official's mendacity went undetected until both he and the mayor had left office is a testament to Giuliani's skill at withholding information.

Harding's father, Ray, had transformed the Liberal Party as its chairman from a dynamic, moderately left-leaning wing of the Democratic Party into a patronage swamp in which ideology ran a distant second. In 1993 the party's endorsement of the Republican Giuliani against liberal Democratic incumbent Mayor David

Dinkins provided the margin of victory in that close election by offering a political fig leaf to disaffected Democrats who otherwise might have remained reluctant to pull the Republican lever. Ray Harding became a key adviser throughout Giuliani's tenure. Another one of his sons, Robert, rose up through the administration to become a deputy mayor.

Robert didn't embarrass his father or the mayor. Russell, though, was a different story. In June 1998, six months into Giuliani's second term, the mayor appointed Russell to run the Housing Development Corporation, a city agency that sought private capital to create low-income housing. He did so despite Russell Harding's absence of experience in this field, as well as his lack of a college degree. Giuliani told reporters he enjoyed getting them upset about such issues because he knew that in the end his judgment would prove sound.

According to federal prosecutors who indicted Russell Harding in March 2003, from virtually his first day on the job he was stealing from the agency. Two years after his arrest, he pleaded guilty to embezzling more than $400,000 through unauthorized payments to himself and improper charges on items ranging from expensive trips to lavish meals. These misdeeds came to light only because *Village Voice* investigative reporter Tom Robbins had been pursuing them since the fall of 2000.

What is most telling and typical of Giuliani's leadership is that Robbins had sent written requests for public information under the Freedom of Information Law, only to be told in June 2001 by Harding's boss, Housing Preservation and Development commissioner Jerilyn Perine, that the records of Harding's spending had been misplaced by a private vendor.

The matter lay dormant until the following February, when Robbins decided to press his request for the records with Harding's successor as HDC president, Charles Brass. A career civil servant, Brass was not able to track down the agency's records of that spending, but he contacted the relevant credit card company, obtained copies of Harding's bills, and forwarded them to the reporter. The stories that emerged produced the federal investigation that led to Harding's indictment and eventual guilty plea.

Brass showed more initiative than Commissioner Perine, but then he wasn't facing the same pressures. By then, there was a new mayor at City Hall—Michael Bloomberg—committed to empowering his deputies and commissioners rather than lording over them. Russell Harding was Perine's direct subordinate, and Perine reported directly up the line to Russell's brother, Robert, a deputy mayor. Perine may have been keenly aware that any publicity about wrongdoing by Russell Harding would displease Giuliani and redound to her detriment. All the same, when the Russell Harding indictment was handed up, Giuliani artfully sidestepped his own responsibility for having appointed an unqualified person (Harding) to a key position, one in which he had remained protected due to this blatant conflict of interest. The former mayor's only comment was given to the *Daily News*, a paper that had virtually canonized him for his stewardship in the wake of 9/11: He told the paper that his "heart goes out to the family."

From Giuliani's time prosecuting corrupt cops as the United States attorney in Manhattan to his first days as a mayoral candidate in 1989, when his unsuccessful maiden bid for City Hall was undermined partly by leaks allegedly orchestrated by a fellow Republican and putative ally, U.S. Senator Alfonse D'Amato, Giuliani developed a comprehensive understanding of the value of information. If knowledge was power, there potentially was as much power vested in withholding information as in providing it. Once he realized the media were unwilling or unable to flex much muscle against a mayor who could exert influence over the business doings of those who owned newspapers and television stations, he also understood that manipulation could be a very potent weapon.

Giuliani had been in office less than five months in 1994 when information surfaced that his Department of Youth Services commissioner, John Brandon, had problems regarding back taxes. As reporters filed their stories that evening, Lategano provided a different spin. She alleged that millions in agency funds that had been handled by Brandon's predecessor, Richard Murphy, could not be located.

With one notable exception (reporter Michael Powell's articles in *Newsday*) the City Hall press corps altered its coverage to give prominence to this new information. Which, unfortunately for them, turned out to be wholly unfounded—a well-timed red herring at the expense of a respected former commissioner whose signature program, Beacon night schools, would be emulated and expanded during the Giuliani years.

For the City Hall media, the administration's changeup was an early insight into the character of Giuliani's governance. There was hardly a ripple in reaction from the newspapers that had been hoodwinked, which also was telling. Giuliani had played the press corps for chumps.

The *Daily News* and *New York Post*, which by being the two loudest newspapers in town often had the effect of driving the local news coverage—including that of the city's radio and television stations—were unabashed Giuliani boosters, for reasons that ranged from their conservative editorial-page ideologies to the business dealings of their publishers. The other two city dailies, *Newsday* and the *New York Times*, were more critical of Giuliani, but didn't share the penchant of the two splashy tabloids for turning a big story into an extended crusade.

As a result, it took time for the public to get over its euphoria at the drastic reduction in crime under Giuliani—aided largely by a burgeoning police force whose costly expansion had been assured by the passage of an income-tax hike under the previous mayor—and register its unhappiness with the way he coarsened the dialogue and trampled the truth whenever it suited him.

Sometimes the administration's distortions were deployed to deal with the most minor headaches. When a man exposed a speed trap operated by cops near the Bronx Zoo, a Police Department spokeswoman told reporters that he had been convicted of child molestation. In fact, the charges against the man had been dropped.

The same type of shift-the-onus tactics were also put into play for more serious situations. After the unarmed Amadou Diallo was killed in February 1999 by undercover cops who, mistaking him for a rape suspect, fired forty-one shots at him outside his Bronx building, detectives swarmed into the building, searched his apartment, and took Diallo's cousin downtown for questioning.

Slightly more than a year later, and shortly after the cops were acquitted, Giuliani responded similarly to the case of Patrick

Dorismond, who was killed after he took umbrage at an undercover detective's request regarding where he could score some marijuana.

The mayor attempted to change the focus in the Dorismond case by releasing Dorismond's juvenile records in order to attack his character. When reporters questioned the propriety of doing so, the mayor responded that legally it was impossible to libel the dead. This posture produced the kind of public revulsion that might have permanently tarnished Giuliani's own legacy if the World Trade Center terrorist attacks had not occurred.

But the Dorismond case was by no means the only time that news coverage reflected the uneasiness of many reporters with Giuliani's way of doing business, whether it was his knack for subtly pumping up racial tensions, his invidious effect on the poor, or his affronts to basic civil liberties.

In spite of the spin peddled tirelessly by the mayor and his band of acolytes, critical reporting surfaced. Tough exposes—some of them in the papers whose editorial boards supported Giuliani at all costs—were published on numerous occasions. But none produced sustained damage to his political reputation the way the municipal corruption scandals of 1986 did for Ed Koch or the Crown Heights rioting in 1991 did for David Dinkins. Much of what was desperately wrong with Giuliani's governance was harder to capture in a headline than could be conveyed about a scandal or a riot.

Giuliani generally treated reporters like unwanted dogs, but there were a few favored puppies in the pack. Dating back to his days as a federal prosecutor, he had shown a willingness to use the well-timed leak when it might benefit him. As mayor, he provided tidbits to reporters who always could be counted on to bury information they received independently about problems festering within the administration.

This year-round climate provided cover to instances of corruption. When a career civil servant named Joseph Trivisonno, who was the deputy buildings commissioner in charge of Brooklyn, enforced city building codes a bit too rigorously for some Orthodox Jewish developers in Brooklyn's Williamsburg section who had supported Giuliani, the developers complained to the mayor's liaison to the Jewish community, Bruce Teitelbaum. As reported by the

Daily News in 1998, Teitelbaum enlisted Deputy Mayor Randy Mastro to pressure Buildings Commissioner Gaston Silva to remove Trivisonno from his post. Eventually Silva took the hint and transferred Trivisonno to another assignment. Then an undocumented laborer from Mexico was killed in a collapse during construction of a different apartment building in Williamsburg by a different Orthodox Jewish developer. Trivisonno went public about his struggles. Giuliani, true to form, responded by accusing him of incompetence.

Brooklyn District Attorney Charles Hynes subsequently launched an investigation into whether City Hall had relaxed building code enforcement to accommodate an important political faction, and at one point his office hinted that Teitelbaum might be indicted. Giuliani hit back with a furious denunciation of Hynes.

The Brooklyn DA finally concluded that the pressure from one group of developers was too slender a thread on which to build an indictment of Teitelbaum for the migrant worker's fatality at a building belonging to another developer. Nonetheless, Hynes later found himself the target of a series of disproportionately harsh editorials on other subjects in the *Daily News*, whose editorial page editor at the time, Richard Schwartz, had been a former senior adviser to Giuliani at City Hall. While it is impossible to assume Schwartz was defending the mayor because of their past ties, reporters at the *News* frequently complained to me that major articles deemed too critical of the administration were killed or banished to the back of the news section by top editors. It was even suspected by some that Giuliani himself was calling publisher Mort Zuckerman to apply pressure. The evident determination of Giuliani and his aides to manage news coverage led one former reporter at the *News* to remark that they "were very aggressive in calling and going above reporters' heads" to influence the paper's portrayals of the administration.

A reporter still with the paper recounted one instance in which Giuliani himself was directly involved: the *News's* attempt to discover in the spring of 2000 whether the mayor was having an affair with a Manhattan divorcee, Judith Nathan, while still married to actress-journalist Donna Hanover, the mother of their two children.

According to this reporter's account, at one point an editor at the paper assigned an intern to stake out Nathan's Manhattan apartment. Early one morning, the intern saw Giuliani exit the building with his bodyguards en route to a day at City Hall.

Giuliani had been careless enough about protecting his privacy that a couple of months earlier he quietly brought Nathan to the Inner Circle show, a reporters' roast that attracts virtually every newspaper and local television news organization in the city. But when he learned of the brewing story, he reached out to a top editor, according to the *News* reporter.

This produced a scene in which the editor, in earshot of much of the newsroom, including the intern who had spotted the mayor, reportedly shouted to one subordinate, "I'm not gonna take the word of a goddamned intern over the mayor of the City of New York!"

But Giuliani's word, it turned out, was flexible. After the story broke, he caused a public stir by proclaiming, during a Midtown press conference, his deep affection for Nathan, touching off an equally public and very angry divorce proceeding with Hanover. His declaration was particularly remarkable because at the time he was in the midst of a circus-like U.S. Senate race against Hillary Rodham Clinton.

Giuliani, who had recently learned he had prostate cancer, soon dropped out of the Senate race. His divorce case produced yet another media extravaganza, during which he demonized his estranged wife in the press through his private attorney.

Giuliani's mania for making himself the story of the day in a huge and complicated city, for managing both access to information and the way that information was conveyed, extended even to what was generally regarded as the high point of his tenure: the leadership he projected after the Twin Towers were destroyed.

Gabe Pressman, the dean of local television news media and the head of the freedom-of-the-press committee of the New York Press Club, had complained vociferously before September 11, 2001, about media restrictions imposed by Giuliani. Those included keeping reporters penned up behind barricades at crime scenes and even parades, and having cops confiscate the press cards of those who tried to defy the restrictions.

The business-as-usual restrictions shifted into overdrive after the terrorist attack, Pressman said, as the police were instructed not to let television crews south of Canal Street, keeping them roughly half a mile from the Trade Center wreckage. "Newspaper photographers figured out that the way to get down to Ground Zero was to hide their cameras and their press cards to get past the barriers," Pressman said. "I kept thinking during this period, what are we missing?"

The mayor argued that the restrictions were implemented for security reasons, to protect the privacy of victims' relatives who had gone to the site to await the recovery of their loved ones, and to insulate police officers and firefighters involved in the recovery operation.

Yet, Pressman noted, high-profile figures ranging from members of the U.S. Congress to national network-news anchors were guided past the barricades and given extensive tours of the site. The federal officials, not coincidentally, were in a position to help secure more disaster relief from Washington DC, while the anchorpersons could offer glowing portraits of a mayor who, despite the widespread Giuliani Fatigue that had enveloped New York City, suddenly appeared to have a bright national future.

"Rudy wanted to control everything," Pressman said to me, describing the weeks following 9/11. "He had two press conferences a day, and everything came from that. He was the center of the universe."

TV news managements did not strenuously protest the limitations on access even when reporters as experienced and respected as Pressman tried to make it an issue. Looking back two and a half years later, he said with exasperation, "Rudy was becoming such a demigod, it became, 'How could you question his leadership?' How could the First Amendment be more important than this mayor?"

In a way, Pressman could have been talking about the former mayor's entire eight years of taking credit for what went right and ducking responsibility for what went wrong. In an age when controlling the message is paramount for any ambitious politician, this may be Giuliani's lasting legacy.

Command
Kathleen Brady

MAYOR RUDOLPH W. GIULIANI was no sooner elected in November 1993 than he began to be upset by a series of events. The first was a fire-bombing on a subway train at Fulton Street in December that injured forty riders and terrified hundreds more. When he appeared at the scene, the fire department, police, and emergency teams each gave him a different story. Giuliani found that no one was coordinating the operation. He became very frustrated when he saw that the police and the fire departments each handled emergencies according to their own protocols, often bumping into each to other.

The second event occurred in Brooklyn in January 1994, a few weeks after he was sworn in. An aged water main burst, flooding dozens of homes in Carroll Gardens, and he heard about it only after he woke up and turned on the television.

International events highlighted the kind of disasters the city might face when in 1995 terrorists used sarin in an attack on the Tokyo subway that claimed eight lives and injured 5,500. After federal agencies warned United States cities to be prepared for similar attacks, New York City officials organized a simulation drill that indicated that the first 125 police officers and firefighters on the scene would have been killed because none of them followed procedures. Moreover, it became obvious that New York City had no established procedures for dealing specifically with terrorist events.

Giuliani, a politician from the command and control school, decided to take personal and visible charge of all emergencies. He revived the Office of Emergency Management (OEM) in 1996. It had been established in 1941 as part of Civilian Defense, but in 1975 its duties were assumed by the police department. Under Giuliani, the OEM had three main functions. First, the OEM Watch Command was to monitor the city's key communications channels, including the radio frequencies of the FDNY and the NYPD. Secondly, the OEM was to improve response to major incidents, including terrorist attacks, by conducting drills and exercises that would involve multiple city agencies, particularly the FDNY and the NYPD. Thirdly, it was to manage the city's overall response to a serious incident. In emergencies, the mayor and representatives from relevant agencies were to report to the OEM center while a field responder went to the scene.

Jerome Hauer, who became the first head of the agency, explained the OEM's purpose simply: "Giuliani wanted an agency that had no skin in the game whether it was a fire or police action. He wanted an office that reported to him, with a commissioner that reported to him, whose sole role was to coordinate the city's resources and to efficiently and effectively utilize them." Hauer, who recalled the news events that inspired Giuliani's desire for his own OEM, had come to Giuliani's attention when Ray Downey, Fire Department battalion chief, recommended him. Hauer, who has a master's degree from Johns Hopkins in public health and is an expert on civilian response to chemical and biological terrorism, was chosen after a review of several hundred applicants.

Giuliani, impatient with most city agencies, referred many types of situations to his new appointee. The mayor did not have faith in the health department, although it had a history of groundbreaking work, including during the AIDS crisis. "He gave us the rat programs to manage," Hauer said. "We did a whole series of things—repairs to Yankee Stadium was something we coordinated. Issues with Shea Stadium, the piers, we handled it all because he knew our staff could get it done. He came to us when he wanted something done well. He recognized early on that we needed our own command center."

The city's existing emergency center at police headquarters displeased the mayor. In early 1994, while trying to coordinate operations during a severe ice storm, Giuliani found that its phones were not working properly. Looking into the matter, he discovered several more things that made One Police Plaza—police headquarters—impossible in his eyes as an emergency command center. It lacked a backup phone system, it did not maintain its power generators. Worst of all, it was vulnerable to hurricane force winds and was in a flood zone. A fact little known to anyone outside the Office of Emergency Management is that after Miami and New Orleans, New York is the American city most vulnerable to damage by hurricanes. Although infrequent, when hurricanes strike the city, they can cause far more damage than hurricanes of similar strength do when they hit the southern United States. While most New Yorkers live in blissful ignorance of this danger, Hauer said that the hurricane threat was a big factor in moving the office of emergency preparedness out of police headquarters and ultimately into the World Trade Center.

"Because police headquarters was not built to withstand strong winds, the emergency center there could be compromised during a hurricane. And the mayor hated going there because it was small. There was no room for him, it was not his," Hauer said. "So in the midst of other activities, such as dealing with building collapses, snow emergencies, heat waves, and everything else, we began looking for a new command center."

Giuliani established criteria for situating his new command center. It had to be within walking distance of City Hall because he did not want to have to travel long distances in an emergency. Hauer's team looked at underground facilities and at aboveground facilities. They looked at space in the Municipal Building, a gargantuan structure near City Hall. They looked at city and private facilities within walking distance of City Hall that would meet the mayor's two other criteria—good security and unobstructed views. "The mayor wanted to put up TV screens so that large numbers of people could see them without columns in the way," said Hauer. They looked at fifty facilities over a period of months. In the meantime, the OEM team operated from scattered offices around City Hall.

Finally, the OEM found No. 7 World Trade Center, a forty-seven-story tower at the northern edge of the complex. Its builder was Larry Silverstein, who would become famous after 9/11 as the owner of the doomed Twin Towers. When No. 7 World Trade Center was completed in 1986, Silverstein had leased the whole building to Drexel Burnham Lambert Group, but Drexel quickly backed out in the wake of an insider trading scandal. A year later, in 1987, the stock market crashed, worsening Silverstein's vacancy problems. However, by the time Hauer and Giuliani looked at it, the building was occupied by the CIA, Secret Service, and Federal Home Loan Bank, among others. "It had excellent security and back-up power generation capabilities. It also had unobstructed views, no columns, so we could put up large television screens," Hauer said. In addition, the Secret Service had analyzed the building; it found that nothing but a huge truck bomb could damage it and even that would not bring the building down.

The city negotiated a lease with Silverstein. Ken Fisher, then head of the New York City Council's Subcommittee on Public Siting and Landmarks, later recalled approving a request to lease office space in No. 7 World Trade Center, but he did not know it was for a new emergency command center. Soon, the city began constructing a $15 million Emergency Command Center with bullet-proof glass to protect it from flying debris and a hurricane wall that could withstand winds of 175 to 200 mph. Although it was located on the twenty-third floor, the press took to calling it Rudy's Bunker, suggestive of the same "siege mentality" that had led Giuliani to encircle the City Hall grounds with highway barricades and to cut off access to the plaza and steps—traditionally New York's political soapbox—to demonstrations and large press conferences.

Renting for $1.4 million per year, the 46,000-square-foot command center included four bunk beds and inflatable mattresses for seventy-four workers who would be on constant call during an emergency. It had 11,000 gallons of stored water, a smoking room for employees, showers, and a kitchen. It had a bug-proof communications system connecting hundreds of city workers via computers with a mapping system designed to pinpoint a disaster's proximity to sewer lines, water mains, and subway tunnels. The center was supposed to be invulnerable and certainly was anything but secret. When it opened in June 1999, journalists noted it was "just a stone's throw" from the ground-level parking garage at the World Trade Center that terrorists bombed in 1993.

Above all, the bunker was a state-of-the-art, high-tech showplace with television screens and unobstructed views of a tireless mayor.

To its credit, the OEM Watch Command's monitoring of Emergency Medical Service data played a role in the early identification and containment of the 1999 West Nile flu outbreak. As for the bunker, its finest night was probably New Year's Eve 1999, when Giuliani had all hands on deck, notably officials from scores of agencies ready to react to any millennium-inspired emergency, be it a "Y2K" computer systems collapse or a terrorist attack on celebrations at Times Square. Happily, order prevailed at midnight when the twentieth century yielded to a new millennium. The only tiny glitch came when the Mayor's political foe Senator Charles Schumer stepped up to the mike to deliver an impromptu speech. The microphone suddenly failed so that no one could hear the senator who, uncharacteristically, flattered Giuliani. Later, it was found that the microphone was turned off before Schumer ever began speaking.

* * *

Of course, disaster did come on September 11, 2001. That morning the mayor was breakfasting at the Peninsula Hotel on Fifth Avenue and Fifty-sixth Street when he was told that a two-engine plane struck one of the World Trade towers. He sped downtown in his Chevy Suburban, past St. Vincent's Hospital where knots of doctors and stretchers awaited the wounded. Wild rumors flew: the Sears Tower in Chicago had been attacked, twelve commercial planes were missing, an estimated fifteen thousand were likely to be killed. As Giuliani neared the World Trade Center he looked skyward and saw a man hurtling from one of the towers into the street below. He learned that the White House and City Hall had been evacuated and that the phones at One Police Plaza were out. Giuliani never made it to his bunker, which was off limits by the time he got downtown. Together with the police and fire commissioners, he quickly moved uptown to establish an emergency command post at the Police Academy.

Meanwhile, the police and fire departments did not know who was in charge of evacuating the towers, but at that point it didn't matter because all communications were down. The obliterated World Trade Center was a major link in the city's cellular transmission and broadcasting services. That link was now dead. Communications were no better than they had been the first time terrorists bombed the World Trade Center in 1993, killing six and wounding scores more. Just as in 1993, communications problems and a lack of coordination impeded rescue efforts. The scale of the disaster was greater, but the rescue glitches were the same.

Although millions of dollars were spent to build the bunker and equip it with the latest in communications, the fire department, first responders in any emergency, had non-working radios because their repeater channel, necessary to operations in high rises, did not function properly. Firefighters did not receive information that was available to police, nor did they hear evacuation orders.

The bunker proved to be useless on 9/11. But Hauer adamantly denies that the command center should have been underground or on street level: "Every water main around City Hall is over 100 years old. If you put a command center underground in that environment, at the end of the day you could have a $13–$16 million swimming pool." Moreover, he stressed that when officials built it, they were focused on a chemical and biological attack like the one Tokyo experienced in 1995. Hauer explained that because most chemicals and biologics are heavier than air, they settle on the ground. "When you are dealing with chemical agents, you want to be at least seven or nine floors above ground. The lower you are, including the basement, the more likely you are to be impacted by chemical or biological agents. We were building against threats we thought were realistic," he said.

But if Giuliani did not want to travel long distances in an emergency, did he really want to have to climb twenty-three flights of stairs? "Who's walking?" Hauer said. "We had generators to run the elevator. We had one generator dedicated to us so that we could go up and down and even if the entire city went out, it would work."

Ah, and that became the rub. A giant, six-thousand-gallon diesel fuel tank was located fifteen feet above the ground floor near elevators to supply back-up electricity to the bunker in the event of a power failure. The Secret Service and Solomon Smith Barney, another tenant in the building, had previously sited other smaller back-up tanks so they could maintain operations during a power outage.

Officials who worked at the Fire Department when Giuliani's command center was built say they warned both the city and the Port Authority, which owns the land on which World Trade complex stood, that the tanks posed a hazard and were not consistent with city fire codes. But as a super-agency of the state, the Port Authority had long claimed (at least before 9/11 investigations) that it superseded city codes and that it was not required to follow them. A frequent target of the mayor's ire for what he called its unilateral and unaccountable ways, the Port Authority green-lighted the flammable repository used to power Rudy's bunker.

After 9/11, a team organized by the Federal Emergency Management Agency and the American Society of Civil Engineers reported evidence of very high temperatures typical of fuel fires in the debris from the building they examined. In a preliminary assessment, they raised the possibility that the diesel was responsible for the fire, which melted steel and undermined the building's transfer truss structure. An hour before it fell at 5:28 p.m., heavy black smoke indicative of a fuel fire poured from the area where the tanks were stored. Like the Trade Towers, No. 7 World Trade Center fell straight down, suggesting an internal collapse. Although the Secret Service study indicated that nothing but a truck bomb could bring No. 7 World Trade Center down, it was destroyed by fire.

In the days after 9/11, much of the steel used in construction of all the World Trade buildings was carted off to scrap yards, but engineering societies moved quickly enough to identify scraps they wanted saved for examination. Volunteers from the Structural Engineers Association visited three recycling yards and the Fresh Kills landfill in Staten Island where they located and studied World Trade Center debris. The Worcester Polytechnic Institute evaluated steel evidence and suggested that sulfur released during the fire may have combined with atoms in the steel to form compounds that melt at lower temperatures.

After the 1995 terrorist attack on the Tokyo subway, the U.S. federal government focused on the threat of biological and chemical attacks. New York City officials did the same, even though the terrorist attacks the city had experienced in the recent quarter century were more conventional. The Armed Forces for Puerto Rican National Liberation, known by its Spanish acronym FALN, made several attacks in the 1970s and 1980s, notably on January 24, 1975, when it bombed Fraunces Tavern, killing four people and wounding sixty others. In 1993 fundamentalist Muslims bombed the World Trade Center, killing six. In 1997 two Palestinians were arrested for planning to bomb the Atlantic Avenue subway station in Brooklyn.

New York City under Giuliani studied Tokyo's experience. It prepared for chemical attack, like the one visited on the Japanese city. It situated its emergency center in a high-rise, justifying that in part because Tokyo had placed command centers in tall buildings. Why then could it not follow Tokyo's lead and prepare a detailed evacuation plan for every neighborhood of its city, including downtown? The evacuation plan for the World Trade Center, devised after the 1993 attack, stopped at the front door. Once people got to the sidewalk, they were on their own.

Government agencies were slow to investigate federal and local response to the 9/11 attacks, but the victims' families eventually forced officials to set up an independent investigation commission. The commission took testimony in New York City in May 2004. Both Hauer and Richard Sheier, who succeeded Hauer and was with Giuliani on 9/11, testified. Hauer had left OEM to work for a consulting firm in San Diego in early 2000. He quickly incurred Giuliani's implacable ire when, as a private citizen, he backed the mayoral candidacy of Mark Green, a Giuliani foe, when term limits prevented Giuliani from seeking a third term.

After hearing their testimony and that of other city officials, commission member John Lehman pronounced New York City's pre-9/11 emergency plan "not worthy of the Boy Scouts." When it was Giuliani's turn to testify the following day, he capitalized on the commission's deference to him by softly chiding, "Our enemy is not each other but the terrorists who attacked us." In response, Lehman, a former Secretary of the Navy, wrote in the editorial pages of the *New York Times*, "It has long been military practice to do a thorough study after every battle to find the lessons to be learned. This does not dishonor the heroes of that battle. In addition to recognizing the magnificent heroes of 9/11, this commission must learn lessons and recommend actions to fix problems. Some will deride this as Monday morning quarterbacking, but it is a necessary duty."

* * *

While in office Giuliani, bellicose by nature, put his energy into fighting hurricanes and human foes (political and anticipated terrorist ones). He was so busy combating perceived enemies and bypassing police and fire commissioners that it never entered his mind to prepare a citywide evacuation plan to help people get out of harm's way. The makeshift rescue operation organized on 9/11 was doomed in part because of the FDNY's poor communication systems. In contrast, those in his useless, flaming bunker were state of the art.

In those who attacked the World Trade Center, Giuliani finally had an enemy worthy of his passion and he led the city through its darkest day. History records other disasters. New York City was nearly destroyed by fire in 1776 and again in 1778. It suffered massive civil disturbances when the Draft Riots erupted in 1863. In 1904, the sinking of the Slocum ferry wiped out a large proportion of the local German community. However, Giuliani managed the city through a calamity that hopefully will never be equaled.

Hindsight is twenty-twenty, as Giuliani has intoned since leaving office and building a multi-million dollar consulting business. But one wonders what the pugnacious Giuliani would be saying if a rival had been mayor on 9/11. What if anyone but the self-involved Giuliani had built a highly publicized multi-million dollar emergency command post near a known terrorist target? What if after being warned for years that New York City was subject to sudden attack, that person never upgraded the fire department's communication equipment or devised a citywide evacuation plan? What if that person had installed a six-thousand-gallon diesel fuel tank at No. 7 World Trade Center, which became the only steel-reinforced high-rise to fall in a fire? Would Giuliani be saying that in placing large tanks of diesel fuel at No. 7 World Trade Center, that person had destroyed his own bunker and helped to bring an entire building down?

Control
Glenn Corbett

THE SEPTEMBER 11, 2001, attack on the World Trade Center unleashed the largest emergency responses in American history. The instances of sacrifice by police officers and firefighters have been well documented and were an inspiration to many people around the world. Rudolph Giuliani, personifying steadfastness, was a focal point of public communication and solace throughout. He will long be remembered for showing courage in the face of unimaginable horror.

Yet it has become clear from technical studies of that traumatic day that the city's rescue operation could have been far better organized. It was burdened by the heavy yoke of political paralysis, technological deficiencies, and emergency-management shortcomings. After reading and rereading the analyses, it strikes me that, tragically, the death toll among those who tried to save the lives of innocents trapped at the weakened and burning World Trade Center was larger than it should have been.

There are several reasons for that, including: New York City's long-running rivalry between the police and fire departments, the "battle of the badges"; the separate rather than unified command posts serving each department; an inadequate radio communication system; and the mayor's decision to place the city's new emergency management center on the twenty-third floor of a high rise building within a complex already known to be the largest terror target in the world.

To consider what went wrong that day is sometimes difficult. The former mayor, who moved on to become a security consultant, preferred to focus on the dramatic story of his experiences and those of his aides on 9/11, on the villains and the heroes of the day. His narrative, which is replete with references to Winston Churchill and World War II, is a potent one, and has fueled talk of his running for higher office. But we should look seriously and carefully at the inadequacies of the rescue operation if we are to improve our readiness in this uncertain era.

While some of these problems that coalesced in the face of the attack on New York had existed long before Giuliani became mayor and had surfaced—in real time—in the 1993 bombing of the World Trade Center, other problems were of his own making. Whatever the case, while public safety was the mayor's forte and focus for most of his eight years in office, critical command-and-control realities both new and old throttled the response on 9/11—with arguably fatal consequences for many of the rescuers whose funerals the mayor dutifully attended.

*　*　*

For decades in New York City, even to this day, the Fire Department and the Police Department have competed for a larger slice of the public safety pie. This rivalry has led the NYPD to expand and duplicate activities that in most cities are associated with the fire service, such as the rescue of people trapped at excessive heights, floundering in bodies of water, and requiring extrication from vehicular wrecks. The overlap was well documented prior to Giuliani's arrival in office in January 1994. In a report issued in 1987, then-mayor Edward Koch's deputy mayor, Stanley Brezenoff, outlined the redundancies in the context of worker productivity. The police department nonetheless went on to shoulder many non–law enforcement functions, treading on traditional fire department responsibilities. The incursions continued after 9/11, with the NYPD expanding into the field of hazardous materials response under the rubric of "terrorism preparedness."

In the late 1990s, in an effort to bring order to increasingly complex and contentious emergency operations, Giuliani created the Mayor's Office of Emergency Management and hired Jerome Hauer, who had run Indiana's emergency management agency, to develop and oversee the new office. It soon created a written protocol for who's in charge at emergency scenes among the uniformed services, while still playing the role of referee at emergency scenes whenever police/fire disputes broke out. While the creation of this agency and the protocol were significant steps forward in organizing the city's response to disasters large and small, it did not get to the root of the serious and systemic issue of duplication of duties because neither NYPD nor FDNY, each with legendarily protective and distinctive cultures, showed any inclination toward working together. Organizational redundancy between police and fire services is nonexistent in most other major cities around the country. In other cities, emergency management agencies play a coordinating and logistical role, not that of an umpire.

A similarly stubborn landscape characterized the city's stammering efforts to improve radio communications. Long before 9/11, radios were a constant issue at emergency scenes. Too many people talking on too few channels led to system overload. High-rise buildings are particularly difficult places to send and receive radio signals because the buildings' structures impede transmissions. In the case of the 1993 bombing of the World Trade Center, the inability of the fire department to communicate effectively was a major problem, so much so that it was pinpointed as such in an after-action report prepared by the department. Yet it was these same radios that firefighters brought to the World Trade Center on the crystal-clear morning of September 11, 2001, four months before the conclusion of Giuliani's tenure in office.

In the interim, between the 1993 and 2001 incidents at the World Trade Center, the Port Authority of New York and New Jersey had installed a radio signal amplifier, known as a repeater system, within the complex. This was the bistate authority's direct response, in all likelihood, to the transmission blockages that arose when terrorists had exploded a bomb-laden rent-a-van in a basement parking garage below the trade center in 1993. But in the same intervening years spanning the Giuliani administration, little was done by the city to try to upgrade the fire department's radio system. The difficult technical issue of providing repeater sites throughout the city so that firefighters could readily transmit and receive messages in all buildings and subways was never really confronted.

On 9/11 the firefighters converging from all over the city at the World Trade Center attempted to use the complex's radio system, first testing it in the lobby of the North Tower. The test indicated that the system was not functional, even though it actually was. A volume control switch mistakenly had not been activated, so the system was of no use at all to firefighters ascending the North Tower, according to The 9/11 Commission Report, which investigated the city's response.

The firefighters were confronting a disaster of immense proportions, much larger than what occurred in 1993. If there was ever a need for a robust communications system, it was now. Yet the communication system at their disposal failed them miserably, likely costing many firefighters in the North Tower their lives. These firefighters climbed the stairs of one of the world's tallest buildings without a reliable means of communicating with commanders below. As they conducted their hazardous work as best as humanly possible, they were disadvantaged: there was no way of their getting word from their commanders about the location of the fire or that the tower was in danger of collapsing.

Tragically, while firefighters struggled to use their inadequate radios, new FDNY radios sat in boxes in a city warehouse. The new equipment, in fact, had been issued to firefighters on March 14, 2001, but it was pulled from service a few days later, after a trapped firefighter's "mayday" message went unheard at a house fire in Queens. A fire company responding to that house fire—not those firefighters at the scene—heard the distress message and contacted commanders who were battling the blaze.

In the ensuing months leading to 9/11, an investigation by then-city comptroller Alan Hevesi uncovered an exclusive "no bid – sole source " contract between the city and the manufacturer of the new radios under the watch of Tom Von Essen, Giuliani's fire commissioner. The city and the manufacturer maintained that the transaction was legal, and there the matter was left, although in a relatively little-known book titled *Radio Silence FDNY—The Betrayal of New York's Bravest*, authors FDNY Captain John Joyce and Bill Bowen alleged additional improprieties on the part of city and the company.

The FDNY's radio communication deficiencies on 9/11 were further aggravated because the fire and police departments maintained separate command posts and communication systems, greatly complicating the emergency response. Giuliani, in his book *Leadership*, claims that it was necessary to have separate command posts so that the police could get telephone lines to protect the rest of the city from attack, while fire officers needed to observe the twin towers themselves. The flaw in this conclusion is that it assumes the response to the World Trade Center was composed solely of the FDNY, when, in reality, the NYPD was also a very important player at the trade center.

Indeed, the NYPD Aviation Unit helicopter had the best view of the immediate damage sustained by the towers. The pilot communicated key information to police officers on the ground—but not to the FDNY. Critical bird's-eye observations could not be shared due to the separate command posts and separate radio frequencies. Interoperability was not in play on 9/11.

Defending the rest of the city from any further attack while the towers burned was certainly a major concern for Giuliani. A significant problem for him was that there was no longer an Emergency Operations Center to use for coordination efforts: his so-called bunker had been built on the twenty-third floor of No. 7 World Trade Center, directly across Vesey Street from the twin towers. No. 7 World Trade caught fire after the fall of the towers and fell, taking the multi-million dollar command center along with it.

Immediately after the collapse of the towers, then, Giuliani grabbed the nearest microphone he could find, that of a television reporter, and took control of receiving and disseminating information flowing out of Ground Zero. The country saw a take-charge mayor, a rock solid leader in stormy seas. His no-nonsense approach in the coming hours and days of uncertainty deservedly evoked national praise. The legend of Rudy Giuliani, "America's Mayor," was born.

* * *

While Giuliani remained the main source of public information, the search and rescue operation at Ground Zero suffered from a significant lack of site control, overrun by an overabundance of well-intentioned, would-be rescuers, including many shock-worn relatives and friends of those missing. There were also significant logistical obstacles and unchecked rumors. Even though the FDNY was put in charge of the monumental effort, fire officials were rarely seen on television and not permitted to hold press briefings. Despite the need for the regular and systematic release of information by the rescue professionals who were performing this operation (as was the case in the aftermath of the Oklahoma City bombing), the fire department played second fiddle to a mayor who was virtually 24/7 front and center.

Problems on the ground reached the boiling point in early November 2001, when a skirmish erupted between police and firefighters at Ground Zero, resulting in the arrest of eighteen firefighters. The firefighters were protesting the mayor's decision to limit the number of firefighters searching the smoldering ruins, in which he cited safety concerns. They were incensed, knowing that many victims were still buried under the smoldering debris. The city's fire service has a long tradition of working tirelessly and incessantly to recover fire victims, and Giuliani was standing in their way even as he was describing them as heroes to the media.

The protests were not limited to bereft firefighters. Victims' family members who had called early on for an investigation of why the towers fell rather than merely burned were upset over the destruction of physical evidence in the form of fallen structural steel beams and columns as a result of the quick launch of work to clear the wreckage. Sally Regenhard, the mother of a probationary firefighter killed at the World Trade Center and the founder of the Skyscraper Safety Campaign, called on the mayor to stop the recycling of the steel. Her calls went unanswered. Nearly all of the steel at the nation's biggest crime scene was reduced to scrap metal.

It was against this problematic backdrop—the battle of the badges, separate police and fire command posts, communication problems, the ill-advised placement of the emergency command center at No. 7 World Trade, and the turmoil at Ground Zero—that Giuliani testified on May 19, 2004, before the National Commission on Terrorist Attacks Upon the United States, or the 9/11 commission. Questions about these and many other issues were on the minds of many who filled the seats in the auditorium in Greenwich Village. But instead of a probing line of inquiry, the audience watched with growing dismay as commission members slathered Giuliani with praise. No hard questions were asked by the investigative panel, " just beach balls," as one listener commented at the time. Chairman Thomas Kean, who was the Republican governor of New Jersey in the 1980s, went so far as to say that New York was blessed because the city had Giuliani as mayor on 9/11.

It was not what many of the victims' families had come to hear. They wanted to know what happened at the World Trade Center and why their loved ones—2,749 people, among them 343 firefighters, 23 city police officers, and 37 Port Authority police officers—died. As the beach ball was tossed back and forth, the tensions in the hall grew exponentially. One particular sore point among many of the firefighters' survivors was a lingering allegation that some firefighters had stayed in the towers despite an evacuation order by a command officer. Giuliani offered that these firefighters, in essence, ignored the order simply because there were still civilians potentially to be rescued inside the buildings. The families, however, believe that many of the firefighters who died never heard the order because of the radio communication problems and that there were very few people left to evacuate below the points of impact when the order was given. Some family members also took exception with the number of people Giuliani continued to state were evacuated, 25,000. The National Institute of Standards and Technology, a federal agency that launched a $16 million investigation of the World Trade Center disaster, estimates that 17,400 people were evacuated from both towers.

The frustration at the hearing boiled over when one agitated audience member interrupted Giuliani's recounting of his experiences on 9/11, screaming, "Talk about the radios!" The room erupted, with many 9/11 victim family members now yelling out to Giuliani and the commission. They wanted accountability and truth. They got fluff instead.

"Stop kissing ass!" I distinctly remember someone in the audience pleading from his seat as Giuliani's testimony came to an end. "Three thousand people are dead!"

A hero in the national dialogue, it's not surprising, nonetheless, that Giuliani has felt the scorn of so many 9/11 families. He was the one individual who had possessed the political clout to protect emergency responders as much as possible in the event of another terrorist attack in the wake of the 1993 bombing. He was the one who could have brought public safety efforts in New York City into the twenty-first century by getting the command structure and interagency rivalries straightened out and by ensuring that the best technology was available.

Ultimately, it was the city's leadership—led by Giuliani—that needed to have prepared the city and its emergency services for that fateful day. In the final analysis, the emergency responders met the challenge head on. It was their leaders who let them down.

Legacy
Kevin Baker

NEW YORK CITY has had two great mayors throughout its long and tumultuous history. They were Fiorello La Guardia and DeWitt Clinton.

Many contemporary New Yorkers would be surprised by one or both of those selections and, above all, by the omission of another— Rudolph Giuliani.

Clinton, after all, is a figure from the distant past, when New York mayors were not even elected, but appointed by the state legislature in Albany. He survives in modern memory as the name of a high school, a park, and a neighborhood. Even La Guardia, the man to whom all modern mayors are compared, is by now a hazy icon to many people.

Yet both men shared two salient characteristics that qualify them as truly great leaders of a great metropolis. Not only were Clinton and La Guardia relentless and effective reformers, but each also realized a transcendent vision for the city they led.

Rudy Giuliani's claim to modern greatness, on the other hand, rests upon his responses to two very different crises during his time in office. The most vivid of these was, of course, the calamity of September 11, 2001. In its aftermath, Giuliani simultaneously rallied and eulogized his city through the most shocking crisis in its history.

It is true that, even here, Giuliani would exaggerate and whitewash his own role, as he did concerning almost every aspect of his administration. It was ultimately the mayor, after all, who should have borne the responsibility for allowing hundreds of firefighters to march into the doomed towers with no effective way of communicating with the outside world—a fact he blatantly misled the federal investigative commission about, telling its members that no such communications equipment could have been obtained and that the firefighters chose to stay in the towers.

* * *

Certainly Giuliani did strike the perfect grace note in immediately consoling a badly shaken city—and at a time when the president of the United States was notably absent. The mayor's speeches and press conferences were composed, sympathetic, and inclusive. They were a sharp departure from his bluster in the months preceding, such as his shamelessly exposing the past of a security guard who had been shot dead for no other crime than *refusing* to buy drugs from an undercover narcotics agent. With 9/11, this supremely energetic, forceful—and increasingly aimless—man had at last found a moment that he could rise to, and his reaction was admirable.

Yet even during the most buffoonish dying days of his second and last term, Giuliani remained a popular figure in many neighborhoods of the city, as he was widely credited with having solved the other, broader crisis of the early 1990s—namely, the proliferation of crime and socially aberrant behavior that was thought to have made New York unlivable.

By the start of the last decade of the twentieth century, the number of murders in New York had surpassed two thousand a year. Public drinking and drug use, fare-beating in the subways, panhandling, graffiti, homelessness, perennially filthy streets, rampant pornography and prostitution in the city's Times Square area, and—most emblematic of all—the unsolicited squeegeeing of car windshields at red lights, were all indicative of how life in the city had deteriorated from the halcyon years just after World War II.

When Giuliani took office January 1, 1994, these problems seemed intractable. Prognosticators predicted a dismal and perhaps apocalyptic future. And yet, more than ten years later—ten years of

Giuliani and his anointed successor—there is no denying that the city is a substantially safer, richer, cleaner, more orderly, and more pleasant city than it has been in a long time. Crime has dropped to levels not seen since the mid-1960s. The homeless have become much less conspicuous. Pornography has been banished to a few back streets, or at least back boroughs. Times Square brims with new development and a positive, family-oriented atmosphere. Even the squeegee men seem to have disappeared. Has Giuliani really brought about a miracle?

Much of how you answer that question depends on who and what you choose to believe about the past. Rudolph Giuliani's success goes to the very heart of political mythmaking in America today and the narrative of the nation over the past forty to fifty years. It revolves, as much of all national politics does, around the myth of modern New York.

* * *

Let us start with a few fundamentals about Giuliani's record and work our way back through the past. To deal with the most salient question first: should Giuliani claim credit for reducing the crime rate in New York?

Andrew Karmen, in his magisterial study, *New York Murder Mystery: The True Story behind the Crime Crash of the 1990s*, notes that every large city in the country, no matter what law-and-order strategy it employed, experienced a steep decline in crime during the decade. Karmen, a professor of criminology, has carefully weighed all of the reasons given for New York's dizzying drop in crime. In the end, he attributes the plunge to a fortuitous confluence of underlying factors. The most important of them was the subsidence of the crack epidemic. In addition, he cites the culling of the ranks of criminals and criminal-aged youth through shootings, a plague of AIDS infections, the simple demographics that marked the end of the baby boom, and a sharp increase in college enrollments of young men. He cites, too, the upturn in the national economy, and the influx of predominantly law-abiding immigrants.

Karmen's study concedes only a minimal contribution to any of the self-congratulatory reasons that Giuliani and his innumerable fans in the media gave for the crime drop, such as the city's new, computer-based Compstat program, which pinpoints crime trends.

For all those who will no doubt scorn Karmen's work without bothering to read it, there is another, even more unavoidable fact that argues against the great-man theory: crime rates in New York were already plunging by the time Giuliani took office.

During the administration of Giuliani's predecessor, David Dinkins, the city murder rate fell 13.7 percent; robbery, 14.6 percent; burglary, 17.6 percent; auto theft, 23.8 percent. These were the most dramatic drops in the city's crime rate since the Second World War. When one considers that it was Mayor Dinkins who pushed through a bold income-tax increase to finance the hiring of six thousand more police officers, it is hard to resist the conclusion that Dinkins, rather than Giuliani, might have become a national figure as a law-and-order mayor had he remained in office long enough to claim responsibility for the results.

But this is straying into the realm of perception. Let's get back to the facts. Giuliani's supporters will no doubt point out that the drop in the overall crime index was even more dramatic during Giuliani's first term—40.5 percent. But Wayne Barrett demonstrates in his investigative biography *Rudy!* that this crash is extremely inflated by statistics. Barrett shows that nearly all major crime numbers were systematically manipulated during the Giuliani years, usually through the downgrading of felonies to less serious offenses, in order to produce better figures.

Meanwhile, as both Karmen and Barrett showed, many benchmarks Giuliani set as measures of success in policing the city actually came up short on his watch. Felony arrests in areas such as weapons possession fell off significantly from the Dinkins years, police response time rose by two minutes, or 24 percent, and by 1998 only 27 percent of felony arrests were leading to indictments, as opposed to 38 percent in 1993, Dinkins's last year in office. If Giuliani was chiefly responsible for the return of lawfulness and order, then how does one explain the drops in police performance, the slower response times, the smaller percentage of indictments, and the like?

* * *

Giuliani's police appointees did not have much to brag about when it came to preserving the rights of citizens they were supposed to protect. "If Giuliani was to bask in the glory of the city's plummeting crime rate, he also had to live with the sting of nationally spotlighted cases of NYPD brutality and rising indexes of cop misconduct," writes Barrett. "Other major cities—like San Diego and Boston—showed that it was possible to get one without the other."

Giuliani's efforts at crime control entailed alienating large numbers of New Yorkers through excessive policing tactics in minority neighborhoods. The practices included constant, random searches of black and Hispanic youth and brutal bursts of police force, such as the gunning down of an innocent young man, Amadou Diallo, by plainclothes detectives.

The mayor's open contempt for civil liberties, his refusal to tolerate almost any dissent, and his bully-boy style was signaled by his participation in a grotesque, drunken police rally-turned-melee near City Hall even before he assumed the mayoralty.

Once in power, his disdain for the discourse of democracy was exhibited relentlessly, whether he was shouting down a reporter asking uncomfortable questions at a press conference, attempting to cut off funds to an AIDS hospice that criticized his health care policies, confronting mourners of the world's AIDS victims with a police sniper perched on the roof of City Hall, intimidating demonstrators by ensuring that they spent as much time as possible being put through the legal system, or summoning an unnerving array of police, helicopters, and other hardware to seal off part of Harlem when a particularly noxious black nationalist insisted on holding a rally there.

All of this indicates that Giuliani's actions were less effective in bringing down crime rates than either the steps taken by his predecessors or the outside influences and trends that he had no control over. But what, then, of all the other accomplishments Rudy would claim for his own in transforming New York? Here again, the facts point to the conclusion that most of the accomplishments Giuliani took credit for can be attributed to outside factors. And many of the accomplishments the mayor can take credit for were realized only through callous actions taken against the city's least powerful citizens.

Despite Giuliani's frantic efforts to grab credit for it, the revitalization of Times Square actually resulted from a massive state-city development effort that began under Governor Mario Cuomo and Mayor Edward Koch and was completed by the Dinkins administration, which persuaded the Disney corporation to make a financial commitment to developing Midtown *before* Giuliani ever took office.

The porn shops and theaters that Giuliani claimed to have turned out were also gone months before Rudy ever got to City Hall. The last graffiti-covered subway car was taken off the line in 1989, the final year of the Koch administration, and the city was remarkably free of graffiti and its streets noticeably cleaner, by the time the Democratic presidential convention came to town in 1992. Even the squeegee men, as Barrett documents, had been permanently removed from their busy intersections by the police department before Giuliani actually came to power.

Many of the poor and homeless, meanwhile, were shunted off to the boroughs outside Manhattan or to distant "edge" cities. Something similar happened in municipalities throughout the country. But in New York the process was at the very least accelerated by Giuliani's fanatical determination to "end" welfare, as he put it in a 1998 address, an effort that entailed cutting off access to federal food stamps whenever possible, slashing funding for shelters and affordable housing, and formulating new requirements that made it so difficult for many of the city's poorest and most ill-equipped citizens that they dropped off the welfare rolls and out of sight.

What became of tens of thousands welfare recipients was not something that seemed to interest anyone in the administration, least of all Rudy Giuliani. He turned a blind eye, in one stroke reversing the city's hundred-year-plus record of pioneering the compilation of social statistics to actually help solve problems of poverty, disease, and social welfare.

Faced, then, with all of these fabrications and distortions, all of this unabashed self-aggrandizement, all of this indifference and bullying on the part of Rudy Giuliani and his administration, one can only say: So what? As a *New York Daily News* reporter once remarked, when I called in to the radio show he was on to protest that Giuliani hardly deserved the credit for New York's dramatic crime drop, "I'd rather be lucky than good." Point taken. After all, big-city mayors are always dependent upon the kindness of state and national governments. Politicians everywhere claim credit for growing economies they had nothing to do with—and are buried by slumps they moved heaven and earth to try to prevent. If Giuliani's policies toward the poor were particularly uncaring and cynical, well, how many leaders have ever done more for the unfortunate than their constituents demanded? If many people of color saw their rights violated by the police, no doubt many were happy to live in a safer city, or as Giuliani put it with typical delicacy when asked by a *Washington Post* reporter what he had done for minorities, "They're alive. How about we start with that?"

It would be ingenuous to claim that Rudy Giuliani was not a great mayor only because he grabbed more credit for his accomplishments than he deserved. Many great politicians are self-aggrandizing and lucky. The reason why Giuliani was not truly a great mayor is that he never possessed a transcendent vision of what New York could be. This was no small failure, but a real squandering of a once-in-a-lifetime opportunity. The money and the mandate were both there and Giuliani had the chance given to so few mayors—to bring about a vision of the city that had never been before. If put to no purpose, power simply dissipates; the true test of all leaders is what they do with their mandate. We must ask ourselves then, what did New York's truly great mayors do with their power?

DeWitt Clinton, during his eleven years as mayor, was an executive possessed of seemingly boundless ambitions and interests. He pioneered free universal education in New York by helping to found the Free School Society, which poured public and private money into schools for the poor and the working class. He oversaw plans for the city's long push up Manhattan Island and the monumental rationalization of the city's development through the imposition of the grid system of numbered streets and avenues. He reformed the public markets, started a city orphanage asylum, and helped found the New-York Historical Society and the Literary and Philosophical Society; he even bolstered the harbor defenses during the War of

1812. Any number of further, farsighted educational and cultural programs were blocked in the city's always contentious political atmosphere, although Clinton did his best to push them through.

Yet above all, as Evan Cornog writes in Kenneth Jackson's *Encyclopedia of New York City*, "As mayor and governor Clinton had a vision of the city's future as a great commercial center, and by means of commercial success he hoped to raise the city to cultural eminence as well."

The means to this end was the grandest, most daring public works project in the history of the United States to that point, the building of the Erie Canal. In one stroke, the canal would link the city through the waterways of upstate New York and the Great Lakes to the immense new resources and markets of the westward-streaming nation. Clinton was not able to fully realize his dream until he was in the governor's chair, but when he symbolically mixed the waters of the Hudson and the Atlantic at the canal's opening in 1825, New York had tied its great harbor to the American heartland. It was a commercial advantage that would never be relinquished, vaulting New York once and for all past Boston and Philadelphia to its position as the country's preeminent cultural, as well as commercial, city.

* * *

Fiorello La Guardia's vision of the city's future was developing New York as a great twentieth-century world city that also delivered the fruits of its labors to all of its citizens. In the midst of the Great Depression he pulled the city out of its fiscal and moral bankruptcy, freeing it from both the bankers and Tammany Hall. He performed the related Stygian labors of reforming the city's finances and cleaning up much of its endemic political corruption. He shook up the police department, chased leading gangsters out of town, ameliorated racial discrimination to a degree with fair employment laws, and recruited the most talented and dedicated bureaucracy the city has ever had. La Guardia, the master builder, created the modern city that we all know, and at the completion of this "Great City,"

New York was fittingly crowned the world's symbolic capital with the arrival of the United Nations.

Riding the wave of New Deal liberalism, Fiorello used state, federal, and city monies to build seemingly endless miles of roads, highways, schools, hospitals, bridges, tunnels, parks, beaches, zoos, playgrounds, and, of course, our first two airports. But all of this Great City building, and all of these reforms, were oriented toward the greater goal of making New York a safe, livable, middle-class and working-class town. It was the Little City that revived and flourished most exquisitely under the Little Flower. As Thomas Kessner points out in his seminal biography of La Guardia, *Fiorello La Guardia and the Making of Modern New York*, the Little Flower put a human heart into the city government and created a New York where, for the first time, collective democracy stood between the individual and many of the exigencies of life.

He built New York's first public housing, moved street peddlers into covered markets, employed hundreds of thousands of desperate men and women in public works projects, and unified and expanded the city's mass transit system to its present size while still maintaining the nickel fare.

All of these reforms were not only humanitarian triumphs, but essential to restoring the city's commercial life. Business became easier, cheaper, and more rewarding in the reformed city. Yet like DeWitt Clinton, La Guardia envisioned all these material advances as not merely ends unto themselves, but as a means toward a greater enhancement of the human spirit.

"All too often, life in New York is merely a squalid succession of days, whereas in fact it can be a great, living adventure," La Guardia once claimed. By the end of his time in office the city was offering the average citizen an almost obscene array of possibilities. Besides the new public beaches and parks, there were free concerts and a great free university. New York was not only the capital of the nation's publishing and fashion industries and the emerging world capital of art, but also a city where, for a very reasonable price, a middle-class person could go see the golden age of American theater, legendary baseball stars and teams, and simply the best jazz that ever was.

What legacy did Rudy Giuliani try to leave behind for the city he loved once he had acquired the political power and rare historical circumstances that would have allowed him to try almost anything? What greater vision of New York did Giuliani have to offer us? The answer is: None.

Giuliani and his fans will take umbrage at this conclusion, but it can be verified readily through even the most cursory examination of the record. Let us look, first, at the physical city, the most obvious realm of accomplishment. Certainly, there was and is no dearth of great building projects still to be undertaken. Giuliani's eight years in office offered a unique opportunity to finally finish, or at least start, a long-awaited, badly needed Second Avenue subway, but there was no serious attempt to do so, nor to make any other over-due additions to the transit system; he didn't even attempt to curb the system's steady fare increases.

Let us turn to the waterfront, an obvious direction for a city that was built on sea trade. There was neither any effort made to restore the city's port and freight facilities, as proponents such as U.S. Representative Jerrold Nadler of New York had long advocated, nor any comprehensive plan to remake the city's derelict waterfronts into new neighborhoods. There was not even an attempt to think about what such a plan should look like.

In the end, no significant public building of any kind took place during the Giuliani administration (probably the first time this has ever occurred in the city's history during a period of great prosper-ity). Giuliani and his aides could not bring themselves to evince much interest even in such popular struggles as the late Senator Daniel Patrick Moynihan's long campaign to remake the main city post office into a new Penn Station. There was so little interest in serious planning at Giuliani's City Hall that, when the federal gov-ernment handed over Governor's Island—175 acres of lucrative real estate smack in the middle of New York Harbor—to the city for the sum of one dollar (with the sole stipulation that the city make some good use of it), the Giuliani administration was unable to come up with anything at all, until Congress nearly snatched the island back.

But perhaps this whole critique is unfair. After all, we live in a very different era from that of DeWitt Clinton or Fiorello La Guardia, and one can hardly have expected the modern Republican Rudy Giuliani to have the same liberal, Great City ambitions as his forebears.

Did Giuliani have, instead, some new, radical, right-wing vision of what the city could be? As it was, his coming to power dovetailed almost perfectly with Newt Gingrich's revolutionary conquest of the Congress and the election of Republican Governor George Pataki, both in 1994. Just as La Guardia was a liberal whose good fortune it was to win the mayoralty in a great liberal era, Rudy Giuliani was a Republican in power at the start of the most thoroughly Republican era in over sixty years. Surely, this was the moment to make New York the incubator of bold, new Republican experimentation, just as La Guardia had let the Roosevelt administration make New York City the showcase of the New Deal.

It didn't happen. One need only to look at New York's public school system under Rudy to understand how he rarely paid more than lip service to his right-wing ideas. Aside from a few noises about school vouchers, Giuliani made no attempt to revitalize the city's schools. Instead, he withheld unprecedented amounts of money from a growing school system for the first three years he was in office and largely contented himself with railing against the Board of Education bureaucracy. He also turned the schools chancellorship into a revolving door—in an effort to enhance his standing within the Republican national party. Even in the months before he wrested the mayoralty from Dinkins, Giuliani connived to get his allies on the city school board to fire one chancellor for daring to allow a school program so audacious as to advocate more tolerance toward lesbians and homosexuals (later rewarding a board member who switched allegiances in his favor with a plum city post). During his years in office, additional chancellors were hired, fired, and tormented regularly, until the position was rendered largely ineffectual. At least this showed a rare, if erratic, involvement with something close to most New Yorker's hearts—the public school system. When it came to most wider issues concerning the city's vital interests, Giuliani often seemed as if he were no more than a moderately interested bystander.

Rather than offend Governor Pataki and other state Republican leaders, he quietly stood by as the state legislature abolished the city commuter tax and severely watered down the city's rent-hike limitations. He genially continued longtime city programs of handing out generous tax breaks to private corporations without any serious study or legal stipulation as to whether they would actually create more jobs. He expressed no trepidation about a city economy that seemed ever more dependent on runaway real estate speculation and stock-jobbing. He seemed, in the end, altogether unconcerned with how most middle- and working-class New Yorkers would find work or get to it, house themselves, or school their children.

* * *

But perhaps it is also unfair to have expected even right-wing reforms—or anything very radical or bold at all. Most New Yorkers remained Democrats during Giuliani's administration—as did the City Council. Could even Rudy really have pushed through a Gingrich agenda in New York?

Maybe, then, the best legacy Giuliani could have left would have been a genuinely conservative one. Couldn't it have been vision enough for Giuliani to consolidate the gains New York had been fortunate enough to make in the 1990s? Reordering its finances, tucking some of its wealth away for the bad times, recruiting outstanding public servants from all walks of life, and reaching out to our city's alienated minorities?

Perhaps. But this did not occur, either. The city's new shimmering surpluses were simply ploughed into expedient operating expenses in the next year's budget. No outstanding new administrators emerged from the Giuliani years, as loyalty to the mayor was valued above all, and an atmosphere of intense paranoia seemed to prevail at City Hall. Virtually no input was solicited from anyone outside the tightly controlled Giuliani coterie. Mayoral aides were terrified to speak on the record even in praise of their boss. Any underling who didn't keep his head down was quickly cashiered. Survivors, on the other hand, were epitomized by the corrupt head of a city-run housing agency, a young man lacking even a college degree, who was hired as reward to his father, the captain of the mislabeled Liberal Party.

In the end, the only part of the city's future that Rudy Giuliani seemed to believe in fervently, the only big and brash new projects that seemed to sustain his interest beyond the immediate formation of the day's headlines were sports stadiums.

In retrospect, that particular obsession seems like a veritable urban mania (and one that has unfortunately overcome his successor, as well). Indeed, over his years in office Giuliani enthusiastically built or promoted a minor-league baseball park at Coney Island that cost $39 million of the taxpayers money and another one on Staten Island that cost $100 million—the most expensive in minor league history.

There were proposals for even more grandiose major-league parks for both the Mets and Yankees and for the Jets, all of which were backed by the mayor. The proposed costs would have amounted to billions of dollars in direct public subsidies. None of the facilities promised to bring even a fraction of the outside dollars that, ironically, Dinkins's revitalization of the U.S. Tennis Center in Flushing did—a facility that Giuliani vilified and boycotted.

Giuliani had no greater vision of the city because all along there was only the vision of the man himself. DeWitt Clinton died in political office. Fiorello La Guardia died two years after leaving the mayoralty—time he spent trying to feed hungry children in postwar Europe (he left a pittance to his widow and his own children). Rudy Giuliani began a wildly remunerative career of speechmaking, consulting, and speculative politicking, no doubt still hoping for the governor's chair, a U.S. Senate seat, a White House cabinet post, or the presidency itself. He left behind a city that was cumulatively better off than when he took power, but it is hard to say if he deserves credit for that.

* * *

A city is not simply a statistical entity, but an aggregation of individuals, and when Rudy took office many of the poorest and most vulnerable people in New York were ruthlessly driven further down the economic ladder. Even during the boom times of the late 1990s, unemployment in New York was higher than the national average and poverty was about twice the national rate. Some 1.8 million

New Yorkers were still below the federal line for severe economic hardship, and given the steadily rising cost of living, their prospects only worsened. Giuliani's legacy was a New York with a steadily diminishing middle class, a city with a much wider gap between rich and poor than anywhere else in the country. Of course, Giuliani himself was not wholly, or even mostly, responsible for this, but that is just the point. He has returned us to a New York that is again almost exclusively dependent upon the vicissitudes of the market-place, especially the dangerously limited and erratic markets of real estate and stock speculation.

For all of his claims to be a radical reformer, Giuliani was a con-summate politician of nostalgia. Herein lies the real secret to his continuing popularity. Giuliani is popular today because he skill-fully exploited the myth of modern New York City.

* * *

Ironically, Giuliani built his winning coalition with a de facto prom-ise to restore New York to the years of the liberal ascendancy before 1965—the city La Guardia built. This is the city that remains golden in the imagination of New Yorkers; more broadly, it is the urban ideal that remains foremost in the mind of America. This is the city of civility, low crime, clean streets, affordable housing, decent enter-tainment, and good jobs at livable wages. It is the city of beloved, dedicated public school teachers, friendly cops on the beat, and racial harmony. That New York City, apart from being a figment of people's imaginations, is a liberal creation. It came into being over the long skein of our history, from the waning years of the Depression to the early to mid-1960s.

Already, in the years just after World War II, America's cities, and not least among them New York, were faced with a burgeoning cri-sis brought about by a perfect storm of changes in American life. Growing middle-class prosperity and seminal gains in civil rights meant both white and black flight from traditional urban neighbor-hoods. The most prosperous, stabilizing families in thousands of communities were suddenly gone, their places taken by masses of relatively unskilled, undereducated immigrants from Latin

America, the South, and elsewhere. At the same moment deindus-trialization brought about the continuing flight of manufacturing jobs from the country in general and the cities in particular, mean-ing the loss of millions of the low-skilled, entry-level but decent-pay-ing jobs that poor immigrants had traditionally used to advance. Rising crimes rates and the proliferation of drugs meant that for the first time in American history cities were not seen as exciting or glamorous places to be, or as places where one stood a better chance of getting ahead. It was liberals who responded to this crisis. It was they who practiced a politics of engagement designed to resuscitate urban America. They had to. They were in charge in the cities.

Of course, they made plenty of mistakes, some of which only made things worse — most notably the Robert Moses–style urban renewal projects that finished off whole neighborhoods. And many of these liberal leaders and politicians were not really liberals at all, only leftover clubhouse cronies, reactionary union leaders, and tyrannical bureaucrats who only paid lip service to liberal principles.

But even the worst excesses of such individuals were challenged, ameliorated, and reversed by grassroots liberal activists and the popu-lar democratic forces they mobilized. To look objectively at the American urban experience of the past half-century following World War II is to recognize an ongoing effort by the leaders and the peo-ples of our great cities to engage problems of housing and homeless-ness, joblessness, drug addiction, and crime. To see what this meant in New York, one need only look at the whole array of long-term efforts referred to above. Putting New York back on its feet has meant Jane Jacobs saving the West Village from the wrecking ball; Mario Cuomo building Battery Park City and using the profits to create middle- and working-class housing; the Cuomo and Koch–initiated rebuilding of Times Square; David Dinkins finding the money to hire more cops; Bobby Kennedy starting a jobs pro-gram in Bedford-Stuyvesant; the Nehemiah and early Banana Kelly projects to rebuild housing by salvaging one neighborhood after another, and so on.

Meanwhile the role of the American right during this struggle to save our cities can best be described as standing off to the side and shooting the wounded. Conservatives have always been, at best, indifferent to the plight of the cities, when they have not been actively hostile. Whether it was Gerald Ford turning his back on New York when it hovered on the edge of bankruptcy, Ronald Reagan cutting almost all funds to build federal housing, or George W. Bush callously and recklessly refusing to let New York City have the money it was promised in the wake of 9/11 for security and rebuilding, the American right has long evinced a philosophy best summed up by that famous *Daily News* headline: "Ford To City: Drop Dead."

This is, when one considers it, a remarkable philosophy for a national political movement. No other major party in modern Europe, or anywhere else in the developed world, has ever advocated simply leaving its nation's cities to molder and rot. Everywhere else in the First World, cities are viewed as repositories of national pride and cultural accomplishment to be carefully cultivated and preserved. In the United States, though, the right long ago found it more politically profitable to cater to a suburbia that is uniquely hostile toward its cities. In order to justify this tactic, the Republican party has perpetuated the myth that all postwar woes of American cities were caused by the people trying to save them—that it was liberal indulgence toward crime and social dysfunction and liberal overspending on welfare and unions that made everyone want to flee to the suburbs. It was the perfect explanation because it exonerated Republicans from the need to do anything at all about cities that, they argued, could only be helped when they decided to help themselves.

Rudy Giuliani was perfectly positioned to exploit this myth and bring about the sort of "toughness" that the right had always claimed to advocate. It was his good fortune to come into office at a time when a number of long-running liberal efforts to revitalize New York were coming to full fruition and when some of the worst demographic trends, such as the crack and AIDS epidemics, were abating. But his appeal, and his administration, were always more about attitude than anything else. The smarmy ads featuring long-time Giuliani friend Ron Silver in the 1993 election were always the vital core of Giuliani-ism. In the ad, Silver's intense, somber presence on the screen looks into the camera and talks knowingly about how the city had declined during the past four years. From his white ethnicity and age to his New York accent, he clearly was to be a kind of spokesman with whom Upper West Side liberals (or at least what the Giuliani campaign imagined them to be) might be able to identify—and his monologue had the stern, inescapable, but ultimately forgiving appeal of a concerned but loving father. Look, it seemed to say, you know and I know that this can't go on. You have elected this unqualified guy (Dinkins), and things are out of control. Straighten yourself up, it's time to clean up this mess. It was a diabolical appeal with a *menschy* face. It played perfectly on New Yorkers' presumed liberal guilt, freeing them to ignore any remaining reservations about Giuliani's actual politics and his Republican credentials. Every problem that New Yorkers had been complaining about for the last half-century or so was now dumped not only onto ineffectual liberalism—but specifically, into the lap of Giuliani's predecessor.

Giuliani's ultimate success was not any actual accomplishment, but his having used the past to move New York City into a future of virtual reality politics. In so doing he followed a national trend. More than ever, politicians in both major parties are judged not on anything they have actually done, but on how convincingly they can invent an imaginary American past from which we can all go forward to a rosy, if carefully unspecified, future.

In the years ahead, New York may or may not flourish, but whatever happens to it will have nothing to do with Rudolph Giuliani. He has called us to no higher purpose. He has charted no new course for us. He has built for us no lasting institutions or even physical improvements.

He has convinced this greatest of democratic cities—the first city ever to be truly run by the people—that all of our great, collective efforts of the past, all of our tolerance and our daring, led only to ruin. He has taught us that all we need is a strong man, and we can leave everything to him. Far from being a great mayor, Giuliani was not even a good one.

Acknowledgments

MANY PEOPLE MADE this book possible, sometimes without even knowing it.

Michael Tomasky had the idea and helped me get started. Sam Stoloff, my agent, assisted immensely with the book proposal. Luckily for both of us, he works for Frances Goldin's literary agency. Frances Goldin played a significant role in the grassroots fight to protect Greenwich Village as we know it from one of Robert Moses's highway projects. She knows a bully when she sees one and (for whatever reason) was receptive to my initial letter of solicitation, which I sent to her at the suggestion of Tom Robbins.

Thanks, too, to Soft Skull Press's intrepid publisher Richard Nash for publishing this volume and to his estimable editing and production staff (Kristin Pulkkinen, Jane Penner, and Sarah Groff-Palermo).

My father, Murray, a writer and editor, read every line of the manuscript and judiciously planted red flags. My mother, Louise, meanwhile, provided encouragement and support from her deep reserves. I am indebted to my parents more than any words could convey.

I covered the Giuliani administration for *Newsday* and for that, too, I feel privileged, in light of the paper's strong traditions of thoroughgoing and independent coverage of government. Tony Marro, as editor of the paper at that time, safeguarded those standards when it wasn't always so easy to do, as did Les Payne, the ranking editor of the New York City edition, and Paul Moses, who was its city editor. Like Paul, Dan Janison, a reporter with whom I worked closely at City Hall, taught me a great deal about the political world—its history, devices, and codes—and taught me to pay the most attention to what politicians do, not what they say.

John Mancini, who succeeded Moses as city editor and later became the editor of *Newsday*, generously supported my goal to put this book together.

Many reporters covered the Giuliani administration fearlessly and persistently; they truly deserve combat pay. Their work, and in particular that which emerged from City Hall's Room 9, inform the these pages.

I'd like to think that *America's Mayor* adds up to something even greater than the sum of its parts. That would be saying a lot, considering the enormous skills of each of its contributors. I happen to know that their participation stems in large measure from their love for New York City and their faithfulness to their own sense of the truth. Otherwise, none would have put up with my pestering.

So many of my friends (they know who they are) were generous with advice, hard-to-find clips, and suggestions. I am lucky, too, that they were patient enough to listen to me.

Finally, I benefited greatly from the insights, encouragement, and love given to me by my wife, Monica McIntyre. I want her and our daughter, Molly, to know I will always be thankful.